THE LUCKIEST MAN ALIVE
The Life of World War I Aviator Captain John H. Hedley

by

Dr. Jack Stokes Ballard

DORRANCE PUBLISHING CO
EST. 1920
PITTSBURGH, PENNSYLVANIA 15238

Dorrance Publishing Co
585 Alpha Drive
Suite 103
Pittsburgh, PA 15238
Visit our website at www.dorrancebookstore.com

ISBN: 978-1-4809-4152-6
eISBN: 978-1-4809-4175-5

CONTENTS

PREFACE

The name Captain John H. Hedley does not appear in the pantheon of World War I aviation giants, such as Manfred von Richthofen, Edward "Mick" Mannock, and Eddie Rickenbacher. Hedley remains a relatively unknown aviator, particularly to generations since World War II. He has, however, a small niche of fame that continues to this day. Captain Hedley, for a long time, has been known as the "Luckiest Man Alive" based on his oft told World War I experience of falling out of his Bristol fighter's observer's seat, free-falling 300 feet, landing on the fuselage near the tail of his own aircraft, and then surviving to a safe landing. As recent as May 2014, the Aviation History magazine noted the Hedley incident as one of "Amazing But True Stories."[1] Thus, Hedley's largely one claim to fame, his signature event, has not faded from aviation lore.

Captain John Hedley's lucky aviation escape story, down through the decades, has no doubt, then and now, challenged belief. The incident was so bizarre it always engendered skepticism. Yet, as Hedley recounted it over and over, it entertained thousands and remained alive reaching a level of acceptance as true. "Believe It or Not" Robert Ripley and Chicago Tribune war correspondent Floyd Gibbons publicized Hedley's account in the late 1920s and gave it national attention in the United States. Hedley capitalized on their news stories with frequent speeches to diverse groups, largely extending outward to the region from his home in Chicago. The presentation of the Hedley story, at one time, became such a dominating force in his psyche that it obviously and drastically changed his life. This book then begins with Hedley's publicized lectures.

As Hedley's life unfolds, many interesting, unsuspecting dimensions appear. Some aspects assume special importance. For example, his major accomplishment of shooting down ten German planes and one balloon make him a World War I double ace. His aerial combat position as a World War I observer, often ignored in histories, proves to be particularly noteworthy. Relatively few histories or publications address the role of the aerial observer. Another Hedley contribution concerns his revelations on the circumstances and plight of a World War I prisoner of war and specifically prison life in Germany's Holzminden prison. As a war prisoner, Hedley struggles, reaching a point of murderous hatred for the prison commandant. Still another unusual aspect of his life develops after he immigrates to the United States after World War I. He aggressively pursues Americanization. The Hedley story thereby opens some new views centered about a British aviator's journey through World War I and into the postwar years.

A flight log, an autobiographical manuscript of World War I service written by Hedley, notebooks, newspaper clippings, and a few letters that Hedley collected greatly facilitates the telling of the Hedley life story. These materials had been handed down to a grandson, Dennis Hedley, who currently lives in Estes Park, Colorado. Fortunately, a considerable number of photographs that Hedley retained help to enrich this volume. While these materials have been indispensable for this history, many information gaps emerge. For example, little can be documented about John Hedley's life while he resided in Los Angeles, California. Even interviews with grandsons Dennis and Don Hedley fail to answer a number of key questions. As a consequence, the Hedley account is replete with his mysterious decisions. Also, complicating accuracy has been Hedley's obvious disregard of documenting events with dates.

Hedley descendants have given crucial family documents and photographs to the World War I museum and archival center of the Lafayette Foundation in Denver. Andy Parks, the head of the Lafayette Foundation, recognized the interesting nature of Captain Hedley's experiences and urged publication of a Hedley biography. Therefore, the tremendous assistance of Dennis Hedley and Andy Parks is gratefully acknowledged. Jean Armstrong of the Wings Over the Rockies Air and Space Museum research library, helped locate British source materials, noted new search areas and critiqued the writing, contributing mightily to this publication. Her assistance has been invaluable and greatly appreciated. Several other individuals, especially Wings museum colleague George Paxton, read and offered helpful comments on manuscript drafts.

Jack Stokes Ballard

CHAPTER 1

The Handbill: "The Luckiest Man Alive"

The bold title on the printed handbill, originating from Chicago, Illinois, read, "Capt. J. H. Hedley: The Luckiest Man Alive." Further it declared a famous war correspondent had applied "The Luckiest Man Alive" label to Hedley. Hedley, a noted World War I air ace, the handbill said, had been secured for the fall speakers' season to give his "Thrillingly interesting lecture 'Rambling Through the Air.'"

Beneath the title and centered on the handbill was evidently a picture of Captain J. H. Hedley, handsomely bedecked in a World War I British Royal Flying Corps uniform complete with RFC wings. Small drawings of World War I biplanes surrounded Hedley. One drawing ominously showed an aircraft going down in flames. A circled sketch to the left of Hedley's portrait depicted an aviator falling out of an aircraft and landing on the tail of the same aircraft. A caption below the drawing stated: "Captain Hedley, three miles in the air, falls 300 feet from his plane, landing safely on tail of the same aircraft."

It was this tidbit of information that triggered thoughts of "Could this be true?" It certainly seemed too bizarre to be true. But this no doubt spurred curiosity and served to increase lecture attendance.

On the backside of the flyer, Hedley, it said, had been a member of the 20th Squadron, R. F. C. (Royal Flying Corps). He took part in some of the most spectacular air fights of the war, having to his credit fifty-three aerial combats. Furthermore, "he fought the famous Richthofen Circus three times …was shot down in flames, and made a prisoner of war." As a conclusive highlight, a final sentence stated, "One of his most startling adventures occurred when he was thrown out of his plane …" and he miraculously survived.

Additional backside paragraphs amplified Hedley's qualifications as a lecturer reporting that he had "joined the British army on August 4th, 1914, on the day war was declared" and served months in the trenches. After working a transfer to the RFC, "He took part in some of the most spectacular air fights on the Western Front, and was officially credited with shooting down twelve enemy airplanes and one balloon."

Besides the war experiences, lecturer Captain Hedley could be expected to "review the history of aviation from the time when man first dreamed of flight" and give "his ideas of the future when airplanes of huge dimensions will be common objects in the sky."

If these statements alone did not pique a reader's imagination, the circular continued, "Captain Hedley is a vastly entertaining speaker and holds his audiences in rapt attention as he tells his unusual personal experiences of the Great War."

As further reinforcement, "Press Comments" were listed at the bottom in small print. For example, according to the Lake Country Times of Hammond, Indiana, "Captain J. H. Hedley, British ace in the late World War, related today with typical Will Rogers humor many of his experiences while a soldier and flyer of the English forces to 200 members of the Hammond Chamber of Commerce. The diminutive ace of the Royal Flying Corps kept his audience in a continued uproar by the manner in which he humorously told of his experiences."

Another report from the Herald News of Joliet, Illinois, stated, "Thrilling and amazing experiences as a British ace during the World War were related by Captain J. H. Hedley of Chicago, at the 'past commanders' night dinner of Harwood Post, American Legion…The largest audience ever to attend a meeting of Harwood post was present, and the hall was filled to capacity."

"The Hall was as still as a June night, with everybody listening to the tales as told by the Captain. The best story teller and biographer who ever delivered an address in Golden Rule Lodge," claimed the Masonic Chronicler.

The Courier-News of Elgin, Illinois, wrote, "Captain Hedley's rare gift of humor kept the audience in a continuous uproar."

Captain John Hedley in his World War I British Royal Flying Corps uniform used this formal photograph in his lecture advertising.

Captain Hedley had this one page "flyer" or "handbill" that he frequently used to promote his lectures.

Thus, this 1928 handbill seemed to capture some colorful selling points for a Captain J. H. Hedley lecture tour. It proclaimed he was a World War I British aerial ace. He had air combat stories even involving the great German ace Richthofen, the noted Red Baron of the Great War. He survived some harrowing experiences such as falling out of his aircraft and being shot down in flames. Even his prisoner of war time was an unusual tale. In addition, he could deliver his accounts in a humorous and entertaining manner.[1]

It is difficult to determine this handbill's distribution in the late 1920s and the geographic spread of the news of Hedley's lecturing. Likely the single sheet, printed in considerable numbers, reached at least hundreds of miles in all directions from Chicago, Hedley's residence at the time. Hedley retained in his personal possession several 8 ½ by 11 metal printer's blocks so he could expeditiously publish additional handbills when necessary. Since the Hedley performance became an advertised part of a "Lyceum Season," that, no doubt, promoted publicity. At this time, the popularity of Chautauqua presentations, including concerts, lectures, and plays, provided a ready-made forum for Hedley's talks. In addition, the lecture notice clearly sought to further oral communication between communities by emphasizing personal or organizational testimonies.

This handbill clearly provided enough intriguing detail to sell Captain Hedley as an interesting person with incredible experiences. His lecture likely would be informative and entertaining. But the questions lingered: Who was this man, this Captain Hedley? Could his advertised heroic and somewhat outlandish stories actually be true or were they exaggerated war commentary, possibly even containing elements of a hoax? What was true and what was fiction? What was this man with such a strong British accent doing lecturing in mid-America? Where did he come from anyway? What was meant by the title "The Luckiest Man Alive"? The answers to these questions could possibly point to a fascinating life story, perhaps even as exciting as a Hedley lecture.

CHAPTER 2

British Cyclist Corps

A ready answer came to the handbill related question, "Where did John Hedley come from?" His accent accurately communicated his British birth and background. More likely than not, the accent helped sell his talks as Americans, hearing his lectures, both then and now, seemed attracted by the quaint speech from across the Atlantic.

John Herbert Hedley was born on July 19, 1887[1], in Tynemouth, England, but his family lived in the nearby town of North Shields. North Shields in Northumberland, not far from the border with Scotland, hugged the English northeast coast near the larger towns of Tynemouth and Newcastle-upon-Tyne. Hedley and others appreciated this picturesque and "wonderfully romantic part of England" where the Hedley's lived. Tynemouth had the ruins of the old Priory founded in the eight century. Tynemouth Abbey, or Tynemouth Castle, as the ruins of the old Priory were often called, stood on a high headland overlooking the entrance to the river Tyne, on the north side of the river. A deep moat thirty or forty feet wide surrounded the Priory grounds with a draw bridge at the entrance. An ancient graveyard occupied part of the area. On the way to Newcastle, a traveler passed through the town of Wallsend. It stood on the site of the Roman camp of Segedunum, marking the east end of the ancient Hadrian's Roman Wall. This rampart ran some seventy four miles across the country with the purpose of defending England's northern frontier from the

Scots. Newcastle itself had a historic cathedral and a ruined castle. During the years of World War I, Captain Hedley sought to counter the misery of war by remembering such details about his home country.

John Hedley's father, Ralph Hedley, worked as a shipyard timekeeper; and his mother, Ann Dunn Hair Hedley, claiming Welsh ancestry, was listed in a census as a shopkeeper. John's father died young at thirty-eight years in 1901; thus oldest son, John, became the man of the family, who would have been fourteen at the time. This no doubt contributed to his maturing more quickly than his two brothers, William Stanley (age eleven) and Ralph (age four). Always small and wiry, he never reached more than five foot-three in height and about 130 pounds in weight. His small stature often made him seem younger than his years, leading to questions about his exact age. During the war, he often would appear a mere boy thrust into fearful military operations.

Hedley attended Queen Victoria High School in North Shields. The school had been built in 1897 and had additions in 1903. Later in his life in Chicago, after he immigrated to the United States, Hedley dedicated a book "to George Bavidge, Headmaster of Queen Victoria Schools, North Shields, England, as a high appreciation of his super human efforts to impart within me the fundamentals of a general education." Hedley attended evening classes at the Western School in North Shields and then Skerry's College in Newcastle-upon-Tyne.[2] This college was one of several of the same name at different locations such as Edinburgh, Liverpool, and Glasgow. The Skerry's Colleges began in 1878 and education focus was on preparation of students for Civil Service examinations. Particular emphasis went to training men for Post Office positions, Customs-Excise Officerships, and other government posts. Little is known about Hedley's academic studies but they likely reflected a mathematics interest. In the 1911 English Census, Hedley's occupation was listed as "Accountant Clerk." Later, he would become a "public accountant" in England working in that career for eight years. Eventually, he would become an auditor and a C.P.A. Energetic and intelligent, he apparently had wide-ranging interests beyond working with figures. He would need to draw on these side interests in order to survive some war episodes, such as his arranging theater skits during his time as a prisoner of war.

On June 6, 1910, Hedley enlisted for four years in the Northern Cyclist Battalion of the Territorial Force.[3] The British military use of bicycles dated as far back as the 1880s. Across the British Isles, volunteer cycle units had been formed with the mission of acting as a "Home Guard" in case of an invasion. In the Boer War, however, cyclists proved valuable in overseas service for reconnaissance and communication purposes. As a consequence, there were approximately 8,000 cyclists by the beginning of the twentieth century. When Britain declared war on Germany on August 4, 1914, entering World War I, there were fourteen cyclist battalions in the Territorial Force. By 1915, these units became the Army Cyclist Corps but the pre-war cyclists still wore their own distinctive unit badges indicating their more humble militia type beginning.[4]

Hedley called his new cyclist unit "The Gaspipe Cavalry." Indeed, by the advent of the twentieth century, bicycles seemed an attractive alternative to horses. After all, cycles, unlike horses, did not require food and water. The bike allowed the soldier to move farther and faster and provided a smaller target. The bike and "cavalryman" would be quieter and more easily concealed. But like the horse cavalry the cyclists could perform key scouting and rapidly carry messages. Moreover, a bike rider could travel as a one-man fighting unit with his "steed" designed to accommodate the rifle and outerwear. A "kit bag" located behind the seat could hold rations and personal items. An emergency tool kit hung on the crossbar. All cyclist members performed minor bike repairs but some were specially trained as mechanics. While the cyclist could use the heavy iron bike effectively and speedily on paved roads, he became far less effective when confronted with muddy, unpaved terrain. When eventually deployed to the Western Front, the cyclist and his bike proved largely unsuitable to the combat conditions and oftentimes evolved into an infantryman. Nevertheless, the British Army had an estimated 14,000 riders in 1914 and 100,000 in 1919.[5]

Perhaps John H. Hedley was a good fit for the Northern Cyclist Battalion. A Captain Trapman of a London Regiment, 25th Cyclist Battalion, declared cyclists made good soldiers, citing their athleticism, quick learning, and education. He assessed army cyclists as "Well educated clerks with a fair percentage of skilled mechanics and tradesmen. Men who in everyday life practically lived on their cycles, averaging 40 to 50 miles a day a-wheel: men who, when they go away for a weekend to the sea in Essex or on the South Coast, never dream of going by train."[6]

The Northern Cyclist Battalion of the Territorial Force was headquartered in Newcastle. Besides acting as a military reserve, it operated primarily as an auxiliary coastguard service for this northeastern English coast. The cyclist battalion as part of the Territorial Force (created as a result of 1908 army reforms), operated as a part-time local defense organization. Members enlisted for a prescribed number of hours over a set number of months. As a result of this "part-time form of soldiering," such enlistees were often termed "Saturday Night Soldiers." Since they were not intended to fight overseas, unless they agreed to do so, they formed a paramount reserve home defense guard.[7] Hedley indicated on his enlistment form that he worked as "clerk" at the John G. Boss Jr. Chartered Accountant firm located at 61 Yeoman Street in North Shields.[8] Thus, he was fully able to be employed as a clerk and do the part-time cyclist soldiering.

Hedley's four year enlistment form specified a requirement for "preliminary training" and a commitment to drills for not less than eight, or more than ten days altogether, in every year. A "mounted unit" stipulation, presumably meaning bicycles, called for not less than eight or more than eighteen drill days in a year. Obviously, these drills would not unduly burden accountant Hedley. After all he was young and vigorous. At that time, he said he was still a teenager, at the age of nineteen years and eleven months.[9] Although Hedley commented he had been discharged from the "5th N. F." at the expiration of two years' service, no documentation has been located about this claimed prior service time. Regardless of the nature of any previous commitment, it seems certain that Hedley's Northern Cyclist Corps enlistment constituted the real beginning of his military experience, limited though it was.

Hedley began training at Camp Almouth from July 24 to August 7, 1910. Apparently he stayed active with his unit and completed the specified drills. His record showed he made corporal rank on June 5, 1912.[10] Later, he became a sergeant and by his contemporaries called "Sergeant Scotty."[11] His rank progression no doubt largely reflected his college education coupled with his intelligence and energy.

In a manuscript that Hedley wrote hoping to get published as a book, partly fiction but containing true insights and events, he described some of his cyclist duty on the Northumberland coastline, centered on the city of Berwick. "In a couple of weeks we had become properly organized at Berwick. Half a dozen men were detached for the local coastguard stations, another dozen each for the coastguard stations located few miles south, at Scremerston and at Gosswick. The balance of the men were assigned for guard duty on the border bridge, and for relief duties at the various posts."[12]

Hedley, and other cyclists, received what he called "old fashioned pre-historic rifles, the long lee-enfield, I think they called them."[13] The men were then pronounced ready for war, said Hedley. Hedley reported men were counted off and given orders to proceed north to Berwick-upon-Tweed and to report to the Harbor Master there. In effect, the cyclists were training to take over duties of the coastguard and the need was great for additional coverage of the coast. Hedley reported the men hopped on their bikes intending to move at the prescribed bike rate of ten miles an hour but with several stops at pubs on the way they arrived at Berwick late, tardiness allegedly caused by faulty maps.

With the beginning of World War I in August of 1914, cyclist duties turned far more serious. Hedley stated there were rumors that a German fleet had left Kiel and it was headed for the British coast. This created alarm and apprehension for the coastguard contingent. "We didn't get such a kick out of the thought of those German warships attempting to land an invasion force, even though we had some trenches, of a sort, ready for our occupation. We had no big guns for defence, not even a machine gun. So the 'invasion' idea wasn't really so very funny," declared Hedley.[14]

There was good reason for some alarm. A German raid on the Yorkshire coast occurred on 15 to16 December, 1914, resulting in a bombardment of the towns of Whitby and Scarborough. There was little damage but there were casualties. The Whitby area had been lightly defended by a single company of the Devonshire Cyclists. They had been ordered to be on alert but with no artillery they were unable to prevent shelling of the coast or to retaliate in any way. Fortunately, the Germans were content with a quick bombardment of the coast and then a hasty escape to German ports.

Some Northern Cyclist Battalion personnel were assigned guard duty on the border bridge. "Things were running along dandy," said Hedley, "We held up every automobile or foot passenger who attempted to cross the border bridge and questioned them as if we suspected them of being German spies. Of course there was plenty of excitement with the work of examination."[15]

On several occasions, a car driver, usually traveling south, would file a report that he had seen flashing lights on a point on Lammermoor Hills, several miles inland but which commanded a view of the North Sea. Spotters claimed these were German spies signaling to German submarines. Supervisors dispatched eight to ten men to ride into the hills to investigate. Hedley had been hauled out of bed for such duty. At first, imagining themselves as capturing spies with a running gun battle, the cyclists became excited but the thrill of chasing spies soon wore off. The suspected spies, claimed Hedley, invariably turned out to be a farmer going his rounds with an oil lamp. The light passing trees and bushes gave the impression of a dot and dash code.

Some of the men, including Hedley, found a convenient barn, far enough from headquarters, to finish off interrupted sleep, resulting from such arduous spy chasing.

Although the Army Cyclist Corps began with Army Order 477, dated November 7, 1914, the Northern Cyclist Battalion continued as an independent unit. The Territorial Force cyclist units were unaffected by the Army Order, including men in those organizations.[16] Upon completing his four years' enlistment in the Northern Cyclist Battalion in June, 1914, Hedley signed papers extending his enlistment in the Territorial Force for two years.[17] Shortly thereafter, on September 23, 1914, Hedley signed an agreement to serve outside the United Kingdom.[18] Obviously with these moves, he was looking ahead to a deeper commitment in British military service.

No doubt the onset of World War I prompted a significant shift in Hedley's life but he had already experienced other major life changes. On December 30, 1912, at age twenty-five, he married Isabella Christina Sands in Tynemouth.[19] Isabella was born on December 25, 1894, in North Shields and thus was seven years younger than Hedley.[20] Hedley remarked that Isabella had been a school classmate, although separated in class years, and they had a young, school-time romance. As a cyclist sergeant, he unexpectedly met Isabella and a date ensued. Hedley described the now more mature Isabella with some notable dramatic flourishes. "Isabella was all rigged up for the occasion. A slender little blonde of nineteen summers and no winters. She looked as gay and colorful as you could wish for. As lovely and enchanting as only a north-country girl could be. Lively, merry, sprightly Isabella…the English duplicate of the Irish colleen who must have inspired the author who wrote 'When Irish Eyes Are Smiling.'"[21]

Hedley believed Isabella was in turn smitten by his uniform and by the sergeant's stripes on his sleeves. Romance was rekindled leading to their marriage.

Two years later in 1914, first son, John Hedley Jr., was born in North Shields. In the same year as Hedley's marriage, his mother died at the age of fifty-three. So, John Hedley, the oldest son with two younger brothers, and a wife and child, had all at once pressing adult responsibilities.

A very young-looking Sergeant John Hedley in the Northern Cyclist Battalion, dated 4 August 1914.

This picture-postcard of Hedley's Northern Cyclist Battalion was mailed to wife "Bella" from Bridlington on 3 August 1914 stating he was breaking camp to go to Newcastle.

Key Hedley Locations

Map of United Kingdom with Key Hedley Locations.

Employed as an accountant-auditor, Hedley projected a business-like image for his employer and clients.

CHAPTER 3

British Army

Having a wife and being a father didn't seem to deter John Hedley from jumping with both feet into the ranks of World War I army volunteers. He was one of many caught up in the patriotic war frenzy that swept Britain at the time. German troops had invaded Belgium and the British government sent an ultimatum to the German Kaiser ordering him to withdraw from Belgian territory or the British Empire would align with France and Belgium to uphold Belgian neutrality. As time elapsed with no German response, people in the British Isles became tense with the excitement of a coming war.

Hedley noted "that even at the end of nearly four months of war there were many people in England who believed the war would be all over within six months. This in spite of Lord Kitchener's (Secretary of State for War 1914-1916) warning that it was going to be a long and tedious job."[1] Many volunteers, perhaps including Hedley, naively believed they needed to get in the army or navy before the conflict ended.

After the war had started and the Northern Cyclist Battalion's full absorption of coastguard-type duties, Hedley and a number of his cyclist companions had become increasingly tired and upset with their home guard role. Hedley indicated frustration even reached the point where they submitted a petition to their commanding officer pleading they be allowed to go to France to fight.

He further told a story, of somewhat doubtful authenticity, about his being involved at the end of 1914 in the "First Footing"[2] custom associated with the New Year's celebration. According to Hedley's account, he and some of his fellow cyclists had been denied leave but nevertheless had gone to their respective homes and communities to participate in New Year festivities. Acting as "First Footers," they became so intoxicated, followed by the hangovers, that they could not promptly return to their posts. Conferencing and contemplating a possible charge of desertion, they determined it was far better to avoid such a possibility by enlisting in the army at the local recruiting station, an army barracks building. On January 3, 1915, Hedley did resign from the Cyclist Corps, listing four years and 188 days service time,[3] and took the oath commencing his army enlistment, more likely for being fed-up with his cyclist duties than the more dramatic circumstances described in association with the New Year. Furthermore, Hedley, it seems, had initiated a request for an officer's commission before his army enlistment. He signed a document, dated December 31, 1914, entitled "nomination of a Candidate for Appointment to a Temporary Commission in the Regular Army for the Period of the War."

Upon his army enlistment, Hedley faced the ever necessary physical. He delighted in telling about problems related to his small size and much later built humor into his lectures about his experiences. Hedley's physical when he enlisted stated his height was five feet-two-and-one-half inches and his weight 116 pounds.[4] Hedley said, "When I joined the Cyclist Battalion no attention was paid to my height, or rather, my lack of height, but when I attempted to join Kitcheners Mob [the army] I found that the minimum height requirement was five feet four inches, and I couldn't make more than five feet two and a half inches in my bare feet. So I was up against it."[5] After stripping naked, he told that he schemed to get by the height standard by first inserting cork soles in his stockings and trying to get by in stocking feet. This failed and he claimed he then succeeded in passing by getting a nasty bump on his head, the size of an egg, by none other than his old family doctor. Hedley said that the doctor turned around and remarked, "Okay, Sergeant Major, take his height and weight before the swelling goes down." This allowed him to scrape by the "machine platform" to the required additional inches. Diminutive Hedley was declared "fit for service."

Hedley also told, with his appropriate British accents, how his small size and his height in particular caused difficulties in getting fitted for uniforms.

When in line to draw clothing, Hedley noticed the Quarter Master kept casting glances at him. As be stepped before the Sergeant, he leaned over a counter and looked him up and down.

With tones of utter exasperation, he hollered out for everyone to hear, "Lord help us, wotscomin now. D'ye mean t'sye they've took you in?"

Hedley replied, "Sure, what's the matter with me?"

"Why kiddo," yelled the Quarter Master, "you've got duck disease, yer legs aint long enuf."

"Well, they reach the ground anyway," Hedley retorted.

He then noted that the Quarter Master took another look at him and "assumed one of those sarcastic grins which only an Englishman can assume with perfection and muttered gruffly 'God Save the King.' Hedley noticed all this caused considerable amusement for the other fellows present."[6]

Hedley's uniform outfitting story continued. Reaching into shelves stocked with British khaki uniforms, the Quarter Master handed one to Hedley saying, "Eer son, tyke it away and doan bring it back, it's the smallest size we ave." The uniform was marked height five feet-six inches, weight 160 pounds. Hedley reported, "I got into it, the pants were a bit tight under the arms and buttoned up about my neck, but they gave me a pair of cloth puttees to wrap around my legs so my feet wouldn't get tangled up with the legs of the pants." He threw away suspenders as he had no further use for them.

After the paperwork, physical, and uniforms, Hedley received orders posting him to the Tyneside Irish Battalion of the Northumberland Fusiliers in camp at Ponteland, a few miles from Newcastle. He began the usual introductory drill and military discipline sessions. Sergeant Scotty of the Cyclist Corps had learned a few things about military life over his four service years. He took advantage of his cyclist experience training cyclist recruits and immediately demonstrated his superior skills on the army recruit drill field. At the same time he noted, with considerable disdain, the problems of getting new men used to the military disciplines of individual and group movements. On several occasions he referred to the men as "Kitchener's Mob"[7] and bemoaned England's overall unpreparedness for war, encompassing the extreme shortage of modern rifles and all sorts of equipment. Hedley's drill leadership, on what he called the Moor at Newcastle, led to his being designated a corporal on his first parade and then in a few weeks to the rank of sergeant. Hedley claimed the army sergeant in charge, soon recommended that he should go to an officer's training course. Since he had already applied for a commission, this no doubt helped expedite matters.

Hedley received favorable endorsements for commissioning and was sent to London for a four weeks officer course. He passed an examination and when he reported back to his unit, he had the key recommendation for a commission in his pocket. His appointment as a Second Lieutenant was dated back to the date of his army enlistment, January 3, 1915. Two months later, he passed examinations for promotion to First Lieutenant. His meteoric rise to rank of Captain occurred in another two and a half months. At that point, Hedley somewhat proudly observed, "he was the smallest officer in the British army."[8]

Now as an officer, Hedley was assigned to the 26th Battalion, Northumberland Fusiliers, also known as the Third Tyneside Irish Battalion, a unit of the Tyneside Irish Brigade. This organization Hedley commented, "Was supposed to consist of all Irishmen from Tyneside." This was in keeping with Kitchener's army being augmented at that time by whole battalions built around men from one trade or profession. The prevailing theory being that troops of common interest and background would serve more harmoniously, knowing each other, and helping each other through the trying periods. The unit, however, said Hedley, had only one sergeant, a half a dozen officers, and about eleven hundred men. Factory buildings and warehouses at Gateshead-on-Tyne housed the troops. Officers, and most married men, were allowed to live at home at night, reporting for duty almost like just going to work. Gradually uniforms and equipment became available as drill took place on streets. Hedley complained they had "old discarded long Lee-Enfield rifles which were only fit for drill purposes." In time, however, training became more standardized, emphasizing digging trenches. Squad drill progressed to brigade and divisional maneuvers.

During this period Hedley had one training diversion. Since he was an accountant by profession, he kept an accurate record of the men's pay accounts for his battalion. This led to correspondence with the Paymaster and the highlighting of chaotic problems with the reconciling of many accounts. Hedley received orders to visit headquarters regarding soldier pay. According to Hedley, a General in the Southern Command announced he was planning to request Hedley's transfer to the Army Pay Corps to systematize the pay department. Hedley discretely said "to Hell with the Army Pay Corps" and succeeded in avoiding that duty and returned to his desired fighting unit.[9]

Captain Hedley commanded a company and like soldiers through the ages groused loudly about the mud and the endless marches and maneuvers. His unit first trained in the northeast and then moved to the Salisbury Plain in the southwest, one of the last postings before going on to France.[10] Brigade maneuvers were usually followed by a sports day in camp. Hedley had quite a reputation as a cross country runner and excelled in some five-mile cross country races. He also gained notice as an outspoken, scrappy officer who would come close to telling Majors and other higher officers to go to Hell. This led to several incidents of his being placed under close arrest as an officer. One event had been triggered by Hedley being ordered to organize and train a divisional cyclist company. He angered other commanders because he sought out experienced cyclists and the best men to form the cyclist unit. A Brigadier strenuously objected to Hedley selecting some of his men resulting in a shouting argument with the Brigadier placing Hedley under arrest for his insolence. A General intervened and a Hedley apology resolved the conflict.

Later, when on the Salisbury Plain, Hedley again was placed under arrest. The incident this time was his commandeering Quarter Master stores, sometimes termed "night requisitioning," to outfit his cyclist company. After ten days arrest, he was released without further disciplinary consequences. He received orders, however, to join a reserve infantry battalion at Hornsea, a seaside town in East Yorkshire.

While still in England in 1915, Hedley narrowly escaped serious injury. The Captain was travelling to London on a motorcycle and as he approached the town of Cholderton, a staff car full of staff officers (brass hats) dashed out of a side road and crashed into his motorcycle. The collision carried Hedley and bike some thirty or forty feet and then threw him into a ditch at the side of the road. Although bloody at elbows and knees, he was fortunate to escape major broken bones. This proved to be another indication of Hedley's toughness.

Late in April 1915 while still on the Salisbury Plain, Hedley's infantry training for the Western Front combat intensified. He summarized his ordeal in a long comment:

"After digging trenches all over England and just as arduously filling them again for some other poor bozo to dig fresh, and being primed on such matters as the exact dimensions of traverses and fire bays, the exact height of the fire step, the locations of dugouts, just how many breaths to take between the act of pulling the pin out of a mills bomb (grenades) and throwing it, how far each man must be apart from the man on his right and on his left when advancing in extended formation, how many steps to run before falling prone to the ground before the next rush, how many blasts of the whistle mean the right section will advance and how many for the left section to advance, the exact positions to be occupied by platoon and company commanders in an advance, and a lot more comic things imparted by officers who had never been off the shores of dear old Blighty, we departed for the 'Great Adventure.'"[11]

As time approached for transport to France, he earnestly sought to learn more about the combat he expected to face. He spent considerable spare time visiting with wounded men at hospitals hearing about their experiences. "1 began to form in my own mind a mental picture of just what that great war was like, but when I actually got into it and into the front line trenches, I think it was a thousand times worse than anything I had ever imagined," he said.[12]

Captain Hedley left the reserve camp in England and reported to the 34th Infantry Base Depot on March 9, 1916, at Etaples in France.[13] The Etaples Army Base, located near that old fishing port in the Pas de Calais region, became known as one of the largest British base camps ever established overseas. Built near railroads, roads, and canals, with relatively quick access to the Western Front, it served as the primary location for funneling troops, supplies, guns, and equipment across the English Channel. The camp also had as many as twenty-four hospitals. At its peak, Etaples housed over 100,000 personnel and it was estimated that over one million British, Australian, and Canadian men passed through the complex. Disease became a problem. As early as December 1916, flu cases developed with high mortality rates.

Hedley spent a very brief time at Etaples and then ordered, whether by accident or design wondered Hedley, to the same battalion of Northumberland Fusiliers which was in the line on the Ypres sector of the front. Hedley reported as a replacement officer. He was greeted by a sneer by the commanding officer as he came to the headquarters behind the front line of trenches. The commander viewed most replacements with disdain. His time at the front had not started well.

A fortunate circumstance for Hedley, however, was his assignment with an experienced, calm, and wise non-commissioned officer. Hedley soon declared that Sergeant Taylor was undoubtedly the most outstanding man in the whole battalion and he relied on his advice and counsel, trusting him implicitly.

"He did not know what fear was and had a happy knack of imparting his sense of fearlessness to the other non-commissioned officers and men," said Hedley. Sergeant Taylor happened to come from Hedley's home town contributing to a close relationship.

Hedley joined the battalion when it was in line at Hooge, west of Ypres. He said that his men were rushed to the support of Canadians. He quickly received a baptism of fire during his first three days and nights as the Germans bombarded the battalion positions. A shell burst in front of a trench where Hedley and Sergeant Taylor were talking, killing several men not more than two yards away. Hedley noted he was too scared to say a word and his knees were literally knocking together. Even though he had not previously smoked, the Sergeant suggested he do so if he wanted to survive. "A good smoke is the only thing to soothe a fellow's nerves out here," warned the Sergeant. From that time forth, Captain Hedley became a committed smoker.

Besides the horror of death always at hand in no-man's land and in the trenches, Hedley battled the lice and the trench rats. "I became acquainted with those great fat lazy overfed trench rats about as big as cats. They lived on the bodies of the unburied dead soldiers. They hung around like house pets, squealing like pigs all hours of the day and night ... Often I would pull out my revolver and place it on the parapet and fire point blank at a big fat rat not more than six feet away," remarked Hedley.[14]

The Captain described learning many duties during his time in the trenches, repairing parapets, barbed wire entanglements, digging holes and burying the dead that oftentimes had to be accomplished after dark. He listened to reports from patrols and outposts and kept telephone communication with artillery batteries. There were gas drills and fixing of sniper posts. Hedley claimed he "took a course of instruction at the snipers' school of instruction at Mont Des Cats, and was made sniping officer for the battalion."[15]

He took note that because of his height he had one advantage when the trench mortars got going and incoming fire was fierce. "I was very proud of the fact that I could walk around with my head erect and my shoulders straight and square to the front, like a real British soldier," Hedley proclaimed. "The big fellows always had to duck."[16]

The death of a trooper in Hedley's company made him "doubt the very existence of a God." Hedley wrote that the shelling one day was nothing unusual, "about a hundred German shells an hour falling on our sector," but one shell suddenly fell a few feet in front of the trench where Hedley and others were talking. Its explosion sent shrapnel flying in all directions with one man hit and the others escaping injury. The soldier struck down died on a stretcher going to the rear. Hedley, badly shaken, said the man had been a next door neighbor with a wife and six children. To Hedley, the loss hit hard. "The one man in the group whose life could least be spared by his wife and children, the cleanest living, most God-fearing man who ever trudged the duckboards in France, was called upon to make the greatest sacrifice any man can make... Can you wonder that some of us at times doubted the existence of a God?"[17] Nevertheless, Hedley's faith, though shaken, was not destroyed.

After approximately three months in the front line trenches, a command crisis arose, leading to confrontation between Hedley and his Commanding Officer. Captain Hedley, from the CO's beginning sneer on his arrival, disliked the Commander and the CO had a similar feeling about Hedley. Hedley ascribed much of the friction to the negative opinions about replacement officers allegedly held by Western Front commanders. The Captain, however, on numerous occasions, expressed the view that the rank and file soldiers and non-commissioned officers were the pride of England but the British officers were a disgrace. The strife between the Captain and the Colonel came to a head under unfortunate circumstances. A German attack on the battalion's sector, preceded by the usual furious bombardment, caught the men by surprise a few minutes before the zero hour for "Stand to" one morning. Aroused by a sentry, Captain Hedley ran out of his dug-out yelling "Stand to, Stand to," meaning all men were to man the firing line. The nature of the German barrage indicated an attack was imminent. Every man had a cigarette in his mouth, hanging on to his rifle with the bayonet fixed, and with grenades (mills bombs) at hand, Hedley reported. As the bombardment lifted, the British troops rushed to the fire steps. Indeed, German soldiers advanced to the right and left flanks through the smoke and haze. Hedley said he issued orders for cross fire with gunners on the right firing at the enemy on the left and those on the left firing to the right. It soon was determined that the Germans were pulling back and the attack had been repulsed. During this attack, Hedley's company commander had been killed and only a short time later an orderly appeared and handed Captain Hedley a note saying that the Colonel had assigned company command to a Lieutenant. Hedley interpreted this as a slap in the face and immediately left the trenches to go to the headquarters to confront the Colonel. In his usual spunky fashion, Hedley said that he was the senior officer and that he would not take orders from a Lieutenant. The Colonel said that was his decision and stated his orders would stand. Harsh, hot words were exchanged and the Colonel charged Hedley with insubordination. Hedley under arrest, next faced a doctor who proclaimed he suffered from shell-shock and was to be ordered home. In the succeeding ten days, Hedley went through several evacuation camps, ending up in Calais with orders to go to the War Office in London. In London, Hedley discovered that he had been found "Mentally and physically unfit for service at the front."[18]

In an interview with a friend in the War Office, Hedley offered his story of his front line experiences and explained his being sent back to England. Hedley alleged that a subsequent investigation of the command of his battalion led to the Commanding Officer being brought home and assigned to a reserve command. Hedley, for his part, spent about three months going from one unit to another. He finally passed a medical exam and then had orders to again cross the Channel and to report to the Officer Commanding the 34th Infantry Base Depot at Etaples, France. After a week at Etaples, Captain Hedley was ordered to return to the front.

Hedley's second time at the Western Front proved far different from the first. He now knew what to expect in the trenches. He had a new unit, the Lincolnshire Regiment, and was a company commander. At first, his new assignment put him in the trenches at Hooge but later, after a time at some rest billets, Hedley went to the front near Arras. There had been heavy fighting down in a valley two or three miles east of Arras.

At another rest billet, this time at Arras, Hedley suffered a period of depression. He saw the trench warfare as a "terrible inhuman carnage" and an "uncivilized unchristian slaughter."

When questioned about his low spirit during his quiet, reflective time, he replied it was "just this God damn war business, getting on my nerves I guess." It happened during this down time that Hedley approached a friend about visiting a nearby airfield at Dainville. Hedley recalled that he had been sitting "watching those airplanes do their stuff." "During the last hour I've seen them take their medicine from Fritz's archies,[19] I've seen two or three scraps, and I've seen two of them go down for the last time, and I've got a feeling that's where I belong," declared Hedley.

Furthermore, Hedley said, "This monotonous life in the trenches has no further attraction for me. This job of killing men wholesale doesn't appeal to me anymore."[20]

On a sunny afternoon, Hedley and friend jumped on a lorry and soon arrived at the Dainville aerodrome. Several planes landed just as they reached the field. They had just returned from a show.[21] Captain "Scotty" Hedley admiringly watched each plane gracefully touch down and taxi toward the hangars. He watched the pilots and observers step out of their respective machines. It happened to be a two-seater squadron.

When Hedley and his friend walked to the planes they noticed the bullet holes collected that afternoon. They noticed the many small square patches dotting the wings and fuselage. Some of the patches had quaint little inscriptions on them such as "A little present from an Albatros." All of this proved especially fascinating to Hedley. He began having visions, he commented, on "scouting around above the clouds, picking your own fights ... dodging Archie, diving on a Fritz machine and shooting him down." Added excitement, he thought, might come from diving on the troops and doing some trench strafing.

Hedley brazenly asked a pilot if he could go up for a ride. He was told to see the Major in command of the squadron. The commander wanted to know if he had any authority from his commanding officer which, of course, Hedley had none. After some haggling, the Major reluctantly directed one of his pilots to take Hedley for a short flight around Arras. Hedley's friend declined such foolhardiness. After approximately twenty flying minutes with Hedley in the observer seat, the pilot landed. The Major inquired how did Hedley like his flight. Hedley's alleged reply was "How about me getting a transfer into the Flying Corps, Major."[22]

Hedley received an explanation of the transfer procedure and an application form from the commander. He needed to get a recommendation from his unit Colonel, warned the Major.

Shortly thereafter, Hedley carefully chose a time to present the application form to his commander. The Colonel, said Hedley, became furious, cursed, and demanded to know if the Captain was ashamed of his battalion. In his anger, he talked of the traditions of the Lincolnshire Regiment and what it cost the government to train an officer for duty in the trenches. The Colonel grabbed the application form, tore it into shreds, and threw them on the floor, saying I shall not recommend your transfer!

Two days after this episode, the battalion moved up into the line again. By all appearances, Captain John Hedley remained condemned to life in the trenches as an infantry officer.

While Hedley liked to tell this story it may actually have been far less dramatic. There is little documentary evidence to support Hedley's account but there is an extremely limited and fragmentary documentary source revealing a Hedley assignment to the British Labor Corps just prior to his transition to the Royal Flying Corps.[23] The how and the why he might have spent time in the Labor Corps remains a mystery. It likely would have been brief.

The British Labor Corps had been formed in January 1917 and was created to perform a myriad of logistics tasks, such as building and maintaining a transportation network, supporting the telegraph and telephone systems, moving equipment and supplies, and manning supply dumps. The Labor Corps grew to some 389,000 men or more than 10 percent of the army's strength by the Armistice. Men, including officers, were often assigned to this duty who had been "medically rated below 'A-1' condition needed for front line service." Hedley never mentioned such an assignment and since the Labor Corps was often viewed as a "second class organization," Hedley's service in it would have been far less glamorous than one he wanted to project.[24]

Captain Hedley's military journey to this point had not been easy. He had endured all the training in England prepping for the ordeals of the Western Front. His training had been long and arduous. He even tried to understand what the trench warfare was like by interviewing the returned wounded men. Throughout this preparatory period he had demonstrated a commendable drive and initiative. Unfortunately, however, his scrappy, bantam-rooster-like character had led to conflicts with superiors and even arrests. His military career as an officer always seemed on the brink of disaster. Yet, Hedley's rather down to earth common sense combined with his energy and his obvious desire for combat caught the eye of some superiors and seemed always to save his officer status. When finally reaching combat in the horrible World War I trenches, he found the way to survive was to rely on an experienced and fearless non-commissioned officer. As time went on, his training, his character, and his motivation to serve England seemed to make him well suited for leading men in trench warfare. But at a critical, depressed moment, Hedley had a taste of an exciting alternative to an infantry officer in the trenches to that of fighting in the skies in one of those flimsy wood and canvas airplanes.[25]

Hedley had remarkable rapid promotion to First Lieutenant and shortly thereafter to Captain. He dated this photograph 16 May 1915. He trained with the 26th Battalion, Northumberland Fusiliers.

Captain John Hedley, now assigned to the 12th Lincolnshire Regiment, B.E.F., sent this card to "Bella" on 13 October 1916. He wrote, "Just a few more photos to let you see how I'm getting on." He added, "We had a football team photographed last Sunday but it hasn't turned out very well. We get them on Sunday so will send 2 or 3 on."

On this football team, Hedley is third from the left in the second row. Athletic events, such as football games, provided some relief from the misery of the front for both participants and spectators.

Hedley, seated at right on the ground, was photographed (undated) with his other unit officers.

CHAPTER 4

Royal Flying Corps

Captain "Scotty" Hedley had returned to the trenches not far from Arras but he had not forgotten his exhilarating flight at the Dainville airfield. After three weeks at the trenches, his unit moved back to a rest camp. Hedley quickly determined that he would again visit the Dainville aerodrome. Arriving at the field, he went directly to the Officers' Mess and met the squadron commander. The Major, since he had not seen a Hedley application for transfer, accused Hedley of changing his mind about the transfer or getting "cold feet" about flying. So Hedley went into a difficult explanation of how his commander shredded the application form and refused to agree to a transfer.

The Major said they badly needed pilots so he would give him another application form, have a doctor administer another medical exam, and then talk to the wing commander to see if they could go over the head of Hedley's CO. Within a week, Hedley was called before the Lincolnshire Colonel who demanded "what is the meaning of this second application?" The Colonel angrily cursed Hedley for going over his head and wrote "Not Recommended." Hedley sadly believed his transfer efforts had been successfully frustrated again. Also, he had reason to believe this might have jeopardized a promotion to Major.

About a month later, the battalion had moved into the line again. One morning, unexpectedly, Hedley was called to the battalion headquarters where the Adjutant handed him a note. The Division Headquarters ordered him to report to Wing Headquarters at St. Omer for flying instruction. Hedley packed within an hour, bade goodbye to his fellow officers, and departed. His Commanding Officer refused to see him but he gratefully knew his twenty-two months at the trenches were over.[1]

As previously indicated, Hedley's exciting narrative leading up to this critical turning point in his life and in his military career may have had some exaggeration and perhaps enhanced for dramatic lecture purposes. Certainly his account did not describe any experience in the British Labor Corps likely occurring about this time.

In Hedley's account of transition from infantry to flying officer, he said that he went by train from Arras, via St. Pol, to St. Omer. Upon reaching the town, he then reported to a nearby aerodrome. There was much activity at the airfield when he arrived. Six aircraft took off for a show. For a while he watched fascinated almost forgetting to see the wing commander. The pilots had walked over and climbed into the rear seats of the planes while observers clambered up into the front. They were flying F. E. 2B pusher-type aircraft. He watched each observer swing his Lewis machine gun around its mounting and then clamp an ammunition drum into position. The pilots waved their hands over their heads, and the mechanics standing by pulled the triangular shaped blocks, by means of ropes, away from in front of the wheels. He watched each machine in turn taxi along the ground and then gracefully ascend into the air as if they might have been going on a peace mission rather than off to kill. When the last machine had gone by and joined the others, he walked over to the orderly room and reported himself present for duty.[2] He had just glimpsed his immediate future.

The RFC wing wanted to put Captain Hedley into combat action as soon as possible. Improved German aircraft arriving at the front in greater numbers and better aerial tactics largely developed by Oswald Boelcke had caused heavy British losses and alarmed RFC commanders in early 1917. In addition, a planned British-French offensive set for the spring required deeper reconnaissance missions. RFC commander General Hugh Trenchard ordered aerial units to go on the offensive on April 4, 1917, five days before the scheduled British Arras ground offensive. With the intense air activity, aircraft losses and casualties increased to the point that the RFC recruited gunners from the infantry. The British lost 245 airplanes, 211 aircrew killed, 108 taken prisoner, and 116 wounded in action.[3] This spring 1917 spike in losses, called "Bloody April," created aircraft and crew shortages lasting many months.

Hedley received orders to begin his flying in Farnborough thus he crossed back across the English Channel. Farnborough was already noted as the home of British aviation and the April 1912 birthplace of the Royal Flying Corps. In addition to the flying training at the large airfield, the RFC had established developmental activities related to aerial photography, bomb dropping, aerial gunnery and meteorology. Also, the Royal Aircraft Factory was located there.

Apparently, from the beginning, the Royal Flying Corps planned to train Hedley as an observer. On August 8, 1917, he recorded in his "R. F. C. 'Army' Observer Flying Log Book" a thirty minute "first flight." The next day he had a cross country flight lasting an hour and forty minutes. In the following days, in an AVRO or RE 8, he recorded log book entries of: "dual instruction-straight flying," "observer gun—target practice," "photo gun aerial combat," "formation flying," "towing target," "target practice—towing target," "cross country observation," and "camera gun & formation flight." He had a total of seventeen hours and fifty-five minutes flying time in August. On August 31, he said that he went to Oxford for "Lectures on Theory of Flight, etc."[4]

Following this introduction to flying, on September 8 Hedley went to Hythe, the No. 1 Auxiliary School of Aerial Gunnery. Hythe, also known as Dymchurch airfield, had been established in 1917 to strengthen aerial marksmanship. Initially, students fired at stationary targets but attention turned to improving proficiency in air-to-air and air-to-ground gunnery. A gun camera had been developed there to assess hitting moving aircraft and at the same time conserving ammunition. During almost the whole month of September, he trained in firing aircraft weapons and also in utilizing aircraft cameras. Typical log remarks included "camera gun & towing targets," "shoot at raft on sea shore," "shoots at silhouette, and towing target," and "aerial photos." His flying total reached fifty-eight hours and forty-five minutes. By the early days of October, Hedley noted that he had experienced "stripping the Lewis Gun in the air" and had more aerial photographs.

He received assignment to the 62 Squadron at Rendcomb, Cirencester, in the middle of October. At this time, he began recording the pilots he flew with and the specific aircraft. A new training element included several "Height" tests advancing from one at 13,700 feet to one of 16,200 feet, the latter on October 23.[5]

At the end of October, Hedley left for France and on November 1, 1917, joined the 20 Squadron at "Cassell, Ypres-Pop Road."[6] The 20 Squadron was an observation unit that employed two-seater aircraft. He would become an observer which he could more easily perform without the more lengthy pilot training. Initially, the Squadron flew the F.E. 2B pusher type aircraft with the engine and propeller behind the wings. The observer sat in the very nose of the machine, like the figurehead on a sailing ship, with nothing between him and space except a piece of thin canvas. The pilot sat farther back toward the center section. They communicated with each other by means of a speaking tube.

This particular pusher aircraft was powered by a 120 hp or 160 hp Beardmore inline piston engine with a speed of 80 mph. Its armament included two 7.62 mm Lewis machine guns, one at the observer position and one at the pilot's, and it had a service ceiling of 9000 ft. Planes in the F.E. 2 series had first appeared on the Western Front in January, 1916, and some served to the end of the war, giving them one of the longest combat records of World War I aircraft. It primarily served as a reconnaissance plane but also occasionally became a fighter and bomber.[7]

Hedley indicated that he flew as an observer in the F.E. 2B but that experience must have been very limited because the 20 Squadron began receiving new Bristol F.2B aircraft as early as August, 1917. The heavier, more powerful two seat Bristols represented a major upgrade in performance and reliability over the pusher F.E.2Bs. With a 275 hp Rolls-Royce engine it could reach a speed of 113 mph and a service ceiling of 20,000 feet. The armament consisted of one fixed Vickers and one rear flexible Lewis machine gun.[8] Since Hedley joined the No. 20 Squadron on 1 November 1917 his combat occurred with this more capable Bristol F.2B, serving as an observer in the rear seat.

Hedley's time with the 20 Squadron did not get off with a promising start. On November 3, his third day with the unit, he remarked, "Flying behind lines crashed in field." The same thing happened on the next two days with the added note of "Dud Engine." Flights became less troublesome as he became familiar with the area terrain, however.

Hedley received some training as an artillery spotter. The reporting of the results of the big gun barrages, sometimes called "gun shoots," required guiding the gunners all through the "shoot." Also, he learned how to maintain communication with advancing infantry, to take aerial photographs, to drop bombs, and to observe and to report ground movement. Special attention went to spotting concentrations of troops, gun emplacements, and supply trains. Of course, if involved in an aerial dogfight, he needed the requisite training on the Lewis gun and firing range experience which he largely received at Hythe.[9]

Apparently Captain Hedley adjusted to flying quite readily. Whether in his position in the exposed front of the F.E.2B aircraft or the rear seat of the Bristol F.2B, he generally overcame any fear of flying. This relative fearlessness equated with his courage in the trenches. Nevertheless, he had unconsciously begun to develop a fear of being burned to death in the air. He had witnessed planes catching fire and falling from the skies. It was not until he actually started flying in the war theater, however, that this fear asserted itself and he realized that he was indeed frightened at the thought of being shot down in flames.

Hedley was not alone in his dread of being shot down in a flaming aircraft. Many pilots-observers expressed a similar fear. A debate occurred among crewmen whether one would jump out of the flaming plane or try to ride it down. None wanted to make that choice. Veteran pilots such as Alan Winslow and Major Raoul Lufbery said they would stay with the aircraft yet Lufbery's death in leaving his burning plane seemed to possibly contradict his belief.[10]

The squadron commander informed Hedley that all new flying officers (pilots and observers) would fly behind the front lines for the first two weeks whenever circumstances permitted it. During this introductory period the new fliers were required to learn the topography of the area near their home base and especially become familiar with various landmarks. This was emphasized so that in the event of a forced landing, as when coming out of a scrap, the pilot or observer would lose no time in locating their position. Hedley was told that compasses took time to settle down after a scrap and the sun might not be visible therefore he would not have time to determine which way was west. Also, owing to the zigzag of the trench lines, flying due west was not always the quickest way into friendly territory. Glancing down at the earth to discern a lake or a prominent steeple for guidance west across the lines could prove to be salvation for a crew. It was stressed that many an inexperienced airman became a prisoner of war and delivered a perfectly good airplane into the hands of the Germans due to not learning the landmarks.

Hedley said, "For a couple of weeks I had been having a great time just flying around behind the lines. I could see Dickebusch Lake like a big jellyfish with its head pointed to Ypres and Zillebeke Lake, an elongated triangle pointing due east, in my dreams. I could draw a map of the northern part of France and accurately locate from memory Courtrai, Tourcoing, Roubaix, Lille, La Bassee, Bethune, and the rest of the towns in the sector. I had learned to know the different churches by the looks of their spires from the air and similarly knew the many other prominent landmarks at sight, in rain or shine, drunk or sober."[11]

The day of reckoning finally came for Hedley, however. The flying orders were usually posted on a bulletin board for the following twenty four hours and Hedley noted he was listed for a sortie the following morning.

Hedley declared, "I barely had a wink of sleep that night. Wasn't a bit sleepy… It was dark when the orderly called me. I got up quickly and wandered sleepily to the officers' mess, my eyes only half open. I sat in the mess while the other fellows came slowly drifting in one by one. I watched them sit down to basins of porridge and large plates of ham and eggs. All I had was a cup of coffee and I had great difficulty in swallowing that!"[12]

A very nervous Captain Hedley went to the preparation room. By now he knew the routine of getting ready for a flight ranging as high as 20,000 feet altitude that created temperatures approaching zero at times. Ten to fifteen minutes would be consumed rubbing whale oil on to the hands, faces, and necks. Then the crews would apply a heavy coating of Vaseline. Hedley noted "whale oil, by the way, is not a substitute for rosewater." A woman's silk stocking would be pulled over the forehead and base of the skull, with legs wrapped around the ears. Ladies silk gloves could be pulled from finger tips to the armpits to provide additional warmth for the arms. Hedley noted that his silken equipment was supplied by the government so they "did not have to visit the ladies underwear department stores to make a purchase."[13]

Crews at times wore a chamois-type leather overall suit. Then they added the large double breasted leather flying coats. On Captain Hedley, "the coat collar would come way up above the ears and the tail down around the ankles." Also, the foot gear included the long flying boots extending from the toes up to the hips with leather on the outside and fleece or sheep wool on the inside. To further combat the cold since they flew missions from 18,000 to 20,000 feet, Hedley indicated the crew did have a wiring system in the clothing arms and legs connected to a generator set up in the center section of the fuselage. This offered some measure of relief with plane supplied heat. A wool-lined leather helmet, fitting closely around the face, leaving only the eyes, nose, and mouth exposed, along with wool lined gauntlets covering the hands, completed the flying uniform.

Hedley rightfully complained that while "wearing all this paraphernalia" he had to clear gun jams in the air. At times, he said, he had to replace a small piece of metal about an inch long, called a stop paul, used on the Lewis machine gun. The stop paul would break in the air due to air pressure on the ammunition drums. Furthermore, anyone removing his hand gauntlet to do the gun repairs ran the risk of quickly getting frostbitten fingers.

After receiving a briefing on the nature of the day's mission, Hedley proceeded to the aerodrome where five aircraft awaited. Ground crews had already been warming up the planes.

Hedley remarked, "as I climbed into my machine my pilot gave me specific instructions about being careful not to shoot away any of our wires in my excitement if we got into a scrap and told me he hated like Hell to take a new observer over for the first time, all of which only served to increase my anxiety. I was beginning to wonder whether I had done the right thing in transferring into the flying corps."[14]

The eastern sky was just beginning to show signs of daybreak when Hedley's plane took off. As the planes climbed they circled above the aerodrome until they finally reached 10,000 feet before heading toward the front lines.

"All the way over I had been scanning the sky on the lookout for the enemy airplanes which I was to recognize by that famous black Maltese cross with its white edges, the emblem of the Iron Cross," said Hedley. "I couldn't see one of them anywhere, and I thanked God."[15]

"We crossed the lines at Passchendaele Ridge and I looked down at that great stretch of country, forty or fifty miles square, without a tree or a house upon it, nothing but mud, mud, mud, and more mud. I began to feel sorry for my younger brother Ralph who was down there, an officer in the Machine Gun Corps. At the same time I congratulated myself for at last having had sense enough to get out of those dirty wet slimy trenches and up into the skies, where it was a nice war that morning," Hedley concluded.

As Hedley flew over the front, he watched the big guns flashing below. They seemed to stretch as far as the eye could see. Hedley thought, "It was a wonderfully fascinating sight."

Suddenly, however, things changed for observer Hedley. "A cloud of black smoke appeared immediately in front of the machine and we sailed right through it. Then a ball of black smoke was under one of the wing tips and another underneath the other. There was a weird shrieking sort of noise that I could distinctly hear above the roar of the engine. I began to get nervous. Perhaps the ship is on fire. I grabbed the mouthpiece of my speaking tube and shouted to my pilot, 'what's all this black smoke around us, is the ship on fire?'"

"Aw Hell," the pilot replied rather angrily, "Don't get scared, that's nothing. It's only those German archie gunners down below, shooting a few of their eighteen pounders at us. It's nothing."

"Oh, is that all," Hedley answered, trying to swallow the lump in his throat.

"In a few moments the sky was black with smoke as a barrage grew up in front of us. The ship was shimmying to beat the band, and my knees were stuttering. Every time a shell burst under the machine my heart almost stopped beating and a cold streak ran rapidly up and down my spine. But I wasn't scared. Hell no … not much anyway," commented Hedley.[16] He had experienced his first aerial baptism of fire.

Although Hedley now had a first taste of the horrible realities of aerial combat, he began his time in aviation totally enthused if not maybe enthralled. At one point he commented, "Flying gives you inspiration. It will arouse your imagination, your emotions, and if you have any romance in your soul at all, flying will bring it up…Sometimes it brings up more than romance."[17] He never lost this love of flying.

Hedley wrote on the back of this photograph: "Just finished a shoot, Vickers machine, lower aerodrome, Hythe, 21 Sept. 1917."

All of Captain Hedley's aerial combat resulting in victories occurred when he was an observer in the Bristol F.2B aircraft. Hedley fired while standing in the rear observer cockpit and this contributed to his episode of falling out of the plane when his pilot made a sudden dive.

Hedley Flights East of St. Omer

Hedley's Flights East of St. Omer.

Captain Hedley rarely had photographs when he had the observer single wing insignias on his uniform.

Captain Hedley had this snapshot wearing a leather flying helmet with goggles.

On 10 September 1917, Captain Hedley, on the right, in a heavy flying coat had a stop at Lympne Aerodrome with Canadian Captain J.F. White.

CHAPTER 5

Aerial Combat 1917

Captain John Hedley's aerial combat began and ended with the 20 Squadron. This Squadron had a relatively long history having formed at Netheravon on 1 September 1915. As the Squadron training began, it moved to Filton and then became operational in January 1916. It happened to be the first in the RFC to be totally equipped with the F.E.2B pusher aircraft. Utilization of the two-man F. E. 2B (later the F. E. 2D) came about partly because of greater demands for aerial reconnaissance. The pilots in the single seat scout aircraft had often been too busy flying their machines to make visual notes or take photographs of the land below. Twenty Squadron, as a consequence, became the RFC's first unit with the designation "fighter-reconnaissance." Deeper reconnaissance behind German lines became its primary mission while still fighting German aircraft and performing occasional strafing and bombing runs.

The 20th deployed to France on January 16, 1916, initially based at St. Omer, but then in February, operating from the Clairmarais aerodrome. There the Squadron served under the command of a RFC Wing with its primary missions of reconnaissance, fighter operations, and fighter escort.

Two of 20 Squadron's most noted victories had occurred in June 1916 when pilot Lt. Harry Satchell and observer, 2nd Lt. T. A. M. S. Lewis, had downed Germany's ace Emil Schafer; and on July 6, 1916, when 2 Lt. Woodbridge had wounded Manfred von Richthofen putting him out of action for months.[1] By August of 1917, the Squadron would proudly claim a total of 203 victories since its first one in February 1916, all from the guns of the F. E. 2B or F. E. 2D aircraft.[2]

During all of 1917 and especially in "Bloody April," the 20 Squadron experienced intensive aerial combat resulting in serious crew losses. The RFC searched urgently for replacements.

In August 1917, rumors began to circulate about a change of machines and soon new Bristol F.2B aircraft arrived. The Squadron operations slowed for a brief time as crews became familiar with the more speedy and powerful Bristol two seater. On September 3, Lt. R. M. Makepeace, who later was to be one of Hedley's pilots, and Lt. Waddington claimed a German Albatros scout as the Squadron's first victory with the Bristol F.2B. Only a few days later, on the 11th, the Squadron Bristols claimed five enemy aircraft brought down. On that day, Lt. R. K. Kirkman, another one of Hedley's eventual pilots, registered his first victory of a future total of eight.[3] The Squadron's era of Bristol F.2B aircraft had solidly begun.

Captain Hedley joined the No. 20 Squadron on 1 November 1917 and was immediately thrust into action as an observer in the rear seat of the Bristol F.2B plane. He increasingly became aware of common problems facing Allied air crews. Hedley called them "natural conditions which were particularly favorable to the Germans." The greatest British disadvantage he declared "was that of having the sun in their eyes most of the time."

"In all our fighting we faced the east, and of course, as the sun rises in the east it was always behind the Germans."[4] He lamented the fact that by the time the sun got to the west it proved of little assistance as the aerial activity predominately took place in the forenoon. Additionally, if you glanced directly into the sun you had difficulty seeing anything but dark specks for ten minutes afterwards. The German aviators on the other hand, said Hedley, "with the sun behind them would have a perfect view of our ships, and by maneuvering so they were always between us and the sun, they could swoop down upon us and start shooting before we realized what had happened." As a consequence, "the successful airman had to be always on the alert and have his finger always on the trigger."[5]

Another problem, Hedley noted, was the prevailing wind in France flowing from the west. "Whenever we got into one of those mix-ups we called cat-and-dog fights, where for the time being a pilot loses all sense of location, we kept drifting over into the territory occupied by the Germans. When we emerged from the scrap we would find ourselves some ten or twelve miles over on the wrong side of the trenches, and had to buck a head wind all the way back again."[6]

"Because of all these reasons, and due to the fact that most of the time we were the aggressors, most of the air fighting took place several miles over on the German side of the trenches. The result was that a greater number of our ships which were brought down landed on enemy ground and the occupants, if they lived, were made prisoners of war."[7]

Being over German lines in an air battle would also complicate credits or confirmations of bringing down enemy aircraft according to Hedley. Claims for downing an enemy plane needed to be independently verified by infantry in the trenches, balloonists, or perhaps a formation from another squadron. Thus the British received no credit at all for any German machines shot down several miles over German occupied areas just because of the lack of confirming reports.

In time, Hedley noted that air fighting at an altitude above 15,000 feet posed a very different proposition to fighting below 10,000. The 20 Squadron flights took place at the higher altitude. He maintained that the physical effort required at the higher altitude was much greater than below owing to the rarer oxygen. "A scrap which lasts only a few minutes at 15,000 or 18,000 feet caused as much fatigue as several hours of labor performed on the ground," he complained. Furthermore, swinging a Lewis gun back and forth in its rigging is just like hauling a nine-inch gun around. Hedley said that when a fellow took part in a couple of good fights at higher altitudes he was always ready to cry enough. "At times we have been so fatigued that as soon as we landed we would go straight to our sleeping quarters and flop down on our cots without having enough energy to even take off our flying clothes. We would drop into a sound sleep, lasting for about a couple of hours. But we always woke up thoroughly refreshed and ready for whatever might come next." Hedley alleged that airmen working at the lower altitudes were able to engage in twice as many engagements and not suffer the same amount of exhaustion. "Four or five scraps a day was not unusual for them," he said.

Still another concern of Captain Hedley pertained to the two man crew in the observation squadron. While in the rear cockpit he had weighed the possibility that the pilot could be killed in the air or even just stunned. In such a situation, he would be at the "mercy of Providence," he thought, if he could not fly the airplane. He determined he would learn to fly. Fortunately, said Hedley, most of the pilots he flew with would allow him to fly the ship back to the aerodrome after a mission, just as soon as they safely crossed over to the Allied side of the trenches.

He relished in telling a story how he managed to wrangle some piloting time:

"We were coming back from a show one morning and as we crossed over Ypres, Lieut. Makepeace waggled the joystick and motioned to me to take control. I carried a spare joystick in my cockpit, so I placed it in the socket made for the purpose, and took control of the ship. Makepeace lay back and rested."

"I stuck my nose down and brought the ship down to an altitude of four or five hundred feet, then set my course to follow the Ypres-Poperinghe road back to Cassell where our airdrome was located."

"Everything was going fine, we didn't mind the bumps. As we were approaching Poperinghe, I noticed a large crowd of Tommies congregated in a field over on my right. Thinking that maybe a German plane had been brought down I kicked on a little rudder, banked round and nosed down in the direction of the crowd. I was flying low over the town and keeping my eye on the crowd curious to know what the commotion was all about and pleasantly discovered there was a soccer game in progress… Suddenly the stick was whisked out of my hand, the left wing went up almost vertically and we spun around on the tip of the other, side slipping almost to the ground."

"I looked at Makepeace. He was shaking his fist at me. I imagined he was furious, but Hell, I couldn't help it. I didn't even know what had happened. I shouted to him that it wasn't my fault, and I tried to take hold of the ship again but he waved to me to take my stick out, and he brought the machine back to the airdrome."

"For the rest of the way home I was inventing every probable and improbable cause of the incident. I knew I would get Hell for it from Makepeace."

"As soon as we landed, Jimmy jumped out of the ship, and in typical, unadulterated army language asked me if I was trying to scare the blankety-blank life out of him."

"I tried to explain it was a pure accident, the ship just went over that way, must have been a gust of wind or something."

"Well I'll be damned, shouted Makepeace, I pulled the bloody ship out of your hands. Do you mean to tell me Scotty you did not see that church steeple?"

"I was simply flabbergasted. I had not seen any church steeple. If Jimmy Makepeace had not been wide awake on that occasion. I guess neither of us would have lived long enough to see a church steeple again. Each of our pay envelopes would have been short the price of an army blanket."[8]

Hedley's pilot in this story, Lt. Reginald Milburn Makepeace, was an experienced pilot credited with thirteen victories up to the time of this flight with Hedley as an observer. Makepeace, although born in Darlington in County Durham in 1905, had immigrated with his family to Canada in that year. While working for the Canadian Pacific Railway, he volunteered for the Royal Flying Corps and received a probationary commission as a second lieutenant on November 17, 1916. He became a pilot of an F. E. 2D with 20 Squadron on June 8, 1917, and claimed his first German aircraft on June 29th. Later, Makepeace and Hedley would team in a Bristol F.2B for a successful engagement against German planes.

The Hedley-Makepeace story regarding his close escape near a church steeple assumed some importance as it may help explain how Captain Hedley came to wear pilot wings. Such informal sharing in controlling the aircraft may have rapidly developed flying skills prior to his formal pilot training.

As the winter of 1917 developed on the Western Front, combat operations declined. During November and December the Squadron claimed only twenty-five enemy aircraft shot down. However, patrols and bombing raids contributed to a high casualty rate. An especially grievous loss occurred on December 2 when Capt. H. G. E. Luchford, a pilot with a record of downing 24 enemy aircraft, was shot down and killed.[9]

As for Captain "Scotty" Hedley, however, November and December 1917 proved to be an active, exciting, and victorious time of combat. He experienced his first time over the trenches on November 15 flying with pilot Lt. Makepeace and he noted in his log "Fought 6 huns." On November 16 and 18, he reported a "Scrap" with one German Albatros listed as out of control at 15,000 feet on the latter date. During the remainder of November Hedley recorded photo missions and "indecisive scrapes." There was excitement, however, as he stated "fog got lost down near Arras." December began with Hedley involved in a fight with seven Pfalz aircraft and "engine trouble." December 3rd, he had two sorties with a dawn patrol and an afternoon one where he said his engine was riddled. Most of his flights took over two hours of air time.[10]

In the morning of 5 December, Sergeant Frank Johnson pilot and Captain Hedley in the rear observer seat took off in Bristol F.2B aircraft number A7144. As part of a formation of nine Bristol Fighters, they flew to an area over Dadizeele. At about 7,000 feet they got into a dog fight with five Albatros Scouts and one Albatros two-seater. The very brief "Combats in the Air" report for that date stated "Bristol Fighter A1744 (Pilot Sergt. Johnson, Observer Capt. Hedley) dived on the E. A., and during the fight the observer fired two drums into one E. A., which went down out of control, but was not seen to crash." Another Bristol Fighter in the formation was credited with shooting down the Albatros two-seater in the same report. [11] This represented Hedley's first aerial victory. Surprisingly in his writings and his talks, he did not describe or elaborate in detail about this momentous event.

The Johnson-Hedley crew, again flying the same aircraft, at 9,000 feet claimed an Albatros D.V "Destroyed" east of Staden at 9:15 A.M. on 10 December. The crew filed the following "Combats in the Air" report:

"A formation of four Bristol Fighters of No. 20 Squadron, whilst on Offensive Patrol, observed 5 Albatros Scouts 2 two-seaters about 1,500 ft. below them just east of Staden. On receiving the signal from the leader [Lieut. R. K. Kirkman was leader of the formation] the whole formation of Bristol Fighters dived on the E. A. formation and No. A7144 (pilot Sergt. Johnson, Observer Capt. Hedley) attacked an E. A., one Albatros Scout, which the pilot shot down with his front gun, and, following it down observed the E. A. Scout hit the ground and turned over."[12]

In a surprising revelation, Hedley actually made flight log entries on December 13 and 16, stating that he had piloted Bristol fighter 7174 for one hour and fifty-five minutes "flying behind lines" in "2 ship escort" and later flying forty-eight minutes in a "practice formation."

In the afternoon of December 22nd, pilot Sergeant Johnson and observer Captain John Hedley flying Bristol Fighter A7144, took off with a formation of seven for an Offensive Patrol. When they reached 11,000 feet over Moorslede they were attacked by seven enemy aircraft. Their "Combats in the Air" report stated "Bristol No. A7144 (Pilot Sergt. Johnson, Observer Capt. Hedley) engaged five E. A., at a range of about 50 yards. The pilot dived firing at one E. A., and put about 60 rounds into it, and this enemy machine then went down completely out of control. About ten minutes later two more E. A. attacked A7144. The observer, Capt. Hedley, fired about 80 rounds into one of these two at pointblank range, and it then burst into flames and fell to earth, at S.28. E. 4.d., and it was seen to be still burning on the ground by the observer." One of the other fighters in the formation confirmed the destruction of an additional Albatros making a total of two destroyed and one "Driven out of control" for the 20 Squadron on the afternoon mission.[13] These two victories represented the third and fourth for Captain Hedley. The very busy Hedley-Johnson tandem garnered four of the twenty five late 1917 Squadron victories. The 20 Squadron as a whole claimed a total of 294 enemy aircraft at the close of 1917.[14]

While this exciting combat at the end of 1917 might seem a fitting climax to close out the year, Captain Hedley chose to end 1917 with a more typical British warbird Christmas season celebration. Hedley and other officers of the 20 Squadron "chartered" a vehicle and "made an exodus to St. Omer" to "put on a large binge" in celebration of Christmas Eve. In a kind of grand finale to the party, some members began doing a juggling act with champagne bottles. They threw them toward each other all the way across the room, making the bottles perform one or more loops in transit. Only about one bottle in three could be caught and soon broken glass littered the floor. The place was in an uproar and everyone wanted to do some sort of performance — all at the same time. One officer insisted upon playing the piano and singing his dirty ditty entitled "Dan, Dan, the Sanitary Man." "Scotty" Hedley climbed on to a table offering to fight any man under nine or over ninety. The proprietor called the military police who conducted the revelers to their car and out of the city limits.

Hedley reported the 20th crewmen got safely back to their aerodrome about four in the morning after twice pulling the car out of a ditch. It rained on Christmas morning with a "thick mizzly kind of rain" that Hedley called "Scotch mist." By eleven o'clock most had had breakfast or as Hedley said, "if a couple of mugs of strong black coffee could be called breakfast." The rest of the morning was spent in the mess recuperating from the night before, or getting into the shape for the night to come.

According to Hedley a "bright fellow" proposed playing a joke on the German airmen. The scheme included taking the "enlarged breakfast cups" stowed under the camp beds for bathroom emergencies and dropping them on the German aerodrome with a cardboard note wishing them a Merry Xmas from the British flying corps. A gunnery officer thoughtfully proposed they make a hole in the enameled cups so they could not be used. "Half a dozen ships" warmed up for the sortie and soon they were ready to go. Hedley claimed that pilot Makepeace and he flew tail and wing streamers to lead the show. The Bristol planes flew low over the selected German aerodrome circled a couple of times and then dropped their presents and "beat it back home." German guns remained silent. Back at their base there was much telling about the joke punctuated with raising of full glasses.

Soon a plane droned overhead. It was a German machine flying straight over the aerodrome. Hedley stated it flew a white flag "which they used to do when they came over to drop messages." The German pilot circled the British airfield at an altitude of a hundred feet, waved his arms wildly in the air, then dropped something and beat it off for home again. British guns were silent. The package was recovered and it was a roll of toilet paper. Hedley declared, "Not for the life of me have I been able to decide in my own mind whether the joke was on us or on them."[15] Although Hedley did have flights on December 29 and 30, whatever the interpretation of the joke, it was the main concluding event for the year 1917, a light-hearted one in stark contrast to the horrific drama usually occurring.

Captain Hedley in the center of the photograph observes gun disassembly.

This fragment of an aerial photograph showing trench lines, location unknown, was included in Hedley's papers.

CHAPTER 6

"The Luckiest Man Alive"

While 1917 ended on a lighter note of raucous Christmas celebrating and trying to play a joke on the German airmen, 1918 began with a return to serious warfare. Hedley had a photo mission, flying at 18,500 feet over Courtrai on January 1, 1918. The next day he had a narrow escape on an Offensive Patrol, with pilot Captain Steele, when their aircraft 4802 had the top right wing smashed by anti-aircraft fire necessitating a landing at Bailleul. This was one of the few times that Hedley reported a hit by the always dangerous archie. On 3 January, Lt. Wilfred Beaver, a young Canadian, claimed the 20 Squadron's first victory of the year when he caused an Albatros C to crash.[1] The following day, pilot Reginald Makepeace and observer Hedley, flying Bristol F.2B A7255 at 17,000 feet, about noon, became embroiled in a battle with eight Albatros Scouts. The narrative of their "Combats in the Air" report contained the following entry:

"Whilst on photo Reconn, four Bristol Fighters were engaged by eight Albatros Scouts about noon over MENIN. Five of the E. A. attacked Bristol Fighter A7255 (pilot-2/Lt. Makepeace, observer-Capt. Hedley). The observer fired 50 rounds into the nearest E. A., at 30 yards range. It turned over and went down completely out of control. The other four E. A. turned away, but attacked again a few seconds later. The observer fired several bursts into each of them in turn at a range of about 200 yards. A broken extractor put the rear gun out of action and the pilot then spun down out of the fight."[2]

This engagement clearly reflected a dreaded problem for an observer like Hedley, a malfunctioning Lewis gun. The pilot wisely beat a quick retreat with his rear gun silenced. At the same time, Hedley's credit for an enemy plane "Driven down out of control" constituted his fifth victory and by World War I accepted standards made him an ace.

Hedley did not stress this milestone in any of his verbal (lectures) or written comments although he likely swelled with pride on joining the ace fraternity. Perhaps the increased aerial activity left him little time to reflect on the event. In time, its importance would be overshadowed or lost in the emphasized counting of total victories.

Hedley's success firing his Lewis machine gun in the rear cockpit in the aerial battles represented but one of a number of his tasks. As an observer, he was the photographer. It so happened at this time that the wing headquarters began demanding more photographs of a section of the country near Courtrai, where the headquarters suspected there was a concentration of troops and supplies taking place. Hedley received orders to be the observer who would take the photos.

Hedley noted that as a photographer he had no sights nor view finders. The camera was stuck in the floor of the observer's cockpit. As a consequence, taking aerial photographs seemed largely a matter of judgment tempered with some experience he said. The plane carried two boxes with each containing eighteen plates, and each plate measuring five by four inches. The plates were set upright and a lever arrangement knocked each plate over as it was exposed. When developed the plates needed to show a half inch overlap so that there was a continuous picture of the area photographed. Hedley said they usually took eighteen photos going east and took eighteen coming back west.

According to "Scotty" Hedley, the Twenty Squadron sent only three aircraft on a photographic sortie. One plane took the pictures and the other two escorted for protection. Hedley said the Germans knew this and whenever three Bristol fighters appeared over their territory they had every available plane in the sky to keep the British ships from getting back.[3]

Hedley stressed that in returning from a photographic show they never tried to use the tactic of sticking the nose down and quickly beating it for home. He said, "There were too many dangers involved, from aircraft, Archie, and machine guns. We always stuck our noses up and began to climb trying to make 20,000 as we crossed the trenches." He maintained that "the higher you are the safer you are, in the air, particularly in air fighting."

54

Hedley's flight crossed the trench lines at sixteen thousand feet and got over Courtrai without being molested, except for the Archies. When Hedley was ready for photographing he informed the pilot so that he would fly level as possible during the operation. He completed the job and signaled the pilot to start for home. They climbed higher as they approached the lines. The crews always felt safer the higher they could get. The 20th planes had not gone far when two formations of Germans began closing on them, nine coming from the north and seven from the south. Hedley pointed out the Germans to the pilot and fired a red Very's light into the air to warn the two escorting ships. The three tried to keep on climbing. It was considered a "fatal move" to stick one's nose down and try to beat it across the lines. The safe thing remained to climb as high as possible and then fight one's way through. "In a very short space of time," said Hedley, "we were right in the midst of these sixteen German scouts and a fight for life began."[4]

Hedley's graphic account continued. "The Germans maneuvered so as to break up our formation and five of them sat on my tail. Then we dove downward, throttle full open. The speed was terrific. I expected every minute the machine would buckle up under the tremendous strain. We must have been doing 250 miles per hour."

"My pilot was trying frantically to dodge the bullets that were crashing through our wings and fuselage, zigzagging, rolling, flipping from side to side, changing course every few seconds.

Presently, the canvas on the sides of the fuselage began to breakaway and was flapping in the air. Those five German ships were trying to anticipate every move we made in their mad endeavor to shoot us down."

Hedley said that he "was jammed up against my Lewis gun, traversing it amongst them, shooting burst into one ship after the other. Down and down we came, from eighteen thousand feet above the earth where the temperature is fifty below zero, to one thousand feet where we flattened out as the British anti-aircraft gunners came to our rescue and put up a barrage between us and the enemy."

After a sigh of relief, believing they might have escaped death, Hedley reported he vomited over the side of the fuselage. "Of course I blamed the sudden change in temperature, together with the intense excitement fighting for my life and that terrific, mad dive to earth. You will understand I was going down backwards all the time. The bums back at the squadron didn't accept my explanation and for a long time jollied me about being sick, especially when they wanted to get my goat."[5]

On the ground men counted nearly a hundred bullet holes in the wings and fuselage. Every one of the thirty six photo plates had been smashed. Both of the escort Bristols had been forced down but they managed to land on the Allied side of the trenches. The crews got safely back to the Squadron aerodrome later.

Apparently Hedley's Lewis gun did not bring down a German scout plane as no claim was made in regards to this flight. This photographic mission which went awry resulted in two German victories, however.

Hedley's narrow escape in the foregoing air battle seemed remarkable to his fellow Squadron officers and to Hedley himself. Considering the continuing losses of high scoring Squadron crew members at the hands of the German squadrons, he undoubtedly was termed "lucky." On 6 January, however, Captain John "Scotty" Hedley earned multi-national attention as the "The Luckiest Man Alive" for an entirely different and quite bizarre episode.

The day began in a normal way. Eleven Bristol Fighters took off from their base near the Somme at 8:30 in the morning on an Offensive Patrol. Hedley flying as the observer with pilot Reginald Makepeace circled aircraft A7255 over the aerodrome while climbing to 10,000 feet. Shortly they headed over Houthulst Forest at 15,000 feet in a huge "V."

The large Bristol formation soon became aware of trouble. Hedley noted, "All at once we discovered 17 enemy scout planes about a mile east." An electric sense of battle hit the crews. "Our pilots began to climb higher, trying to gain an advantage for the moment when we would be in the thick of things. The Germans, already higher than we were, also began to pull their noses up for more altitude. Closer and closer they came."

Hedley said, "The odds were against us." Makepeace thought so too as he cut the motor for a second and shouted at Hedley. "If you never prayed in your life before, you'd better begin now."

Hedley indicated he yelled back at Makepeace "What we gotta do is fight; God helps those who help themselves."

The British elected to be the aggressors and to initiate the fight with Hedley saying, "Then we dived into the attack." He further remarked, "The sky seemed full of ships. The German squadron broke up its formation. Some of them tried to single us out as easy meat. The roar of 28 planes, twisting, diving, zooming and banking with wide open motors was deafening. Yet above it all you could hear the stuttering machine guns."

"Lead kept pounding on to our wings and fuselage. Every now and then it seemed to go cracking just clear of my head. I was standing up in the cockpit, firing at every German ship that came within range." This last Hedley comment indicated how vulnerable the observer must have felt standing in the open cockpit, firing when able, and desperately holding on to the gun and ring with violent maneuvers.

As the air battle raged Hedley dramatically described results. "A puff of black smoke, a burst of flame leaping into the air, as ship after ship, ours and the Germans, spun toward the ground. I saw one pilot leap out of his burning plane, arms and legs stretched out, his body making a series of cartwheels as he plunged to his death. The fight lasted 10 or 15 minutes. I thought it would never end. We lost two planes, the Germans five."

"We began to streak for home since our gasoline was running low and we had had our fill. We were then up 20,000 feet."[6]

Captain Hedley and Captain Makepeace probably thought and hoped they had survived this big battle but they were to come under another attack. Hedley said, "Suddenly I noticed an enemy ship, a Fokker, swooping right down upon us."

Then Hedley's amazing feat began to unfold and he best described in detail what happened next in the following scripted radio broadcast:

"He was about sixty feet above us and fifty or sixty feet behind. From the angle of approach I figured the German pilot couldn't see us. Instinctively, I swang my Lewis gun around to take a shot at him. Then the thought flashed through my mind if I shoot his plane will fall to pieces, come down on us and we'll go down with it. If I don't shoot, his landing gear will foul one of our wings and we'll go down anyway. We had a prearranged signal in case of an emergency at the tail of the machine where the observer merely had to bend his head back and tap the pilot on the back of his head. That was a signal to the pilot to make a quick getaway, give her the gun, and beat it for home. On this occasion, in the excitement of battle, I threw my head back so violently that the pilot got a shock. He pushed his stick forward as far as it would go and the ship went down into a vertical power dive catapulting me into the air. As this happened I think I must have held on to the gun and as the ship lurched downward it dragged me behind headfirst. Then I lost consciousness, my grip was broken, and I continued to fall fifteen or twenty feet behind the plane. After diving three or five hundred feet my pilot straightened out into level flight. As he did so, I landed on the tail end and stuck there."

"Makepeace, my pilot, had no idea that I was out of the cockpit. He felt the jar on the tail end and thought another plane had collided with us until he looked around and saw me squatted out there. I clearly recall my sensations. I knew the ship had gone into the dive then everything became black. I thought I was falling through space. On second thought, because everything was so dark, I figured I must be dead. Then putting my hands up to my eyes I discovered that the face opening of my flying helmet was at the back of my head. I adjusted it then discovered I was sitting straddle legged on the tail of the ship facing the rudder and close enough to touch it."

"I looked around to my pilot. He was waving vigorously for me to come back into my own office. For a few moments I wondered what was best to do — hang on until Makepeace could get the ship back to earth or climb back to my cockpit. The fuselage looked at least a mile and a half long. If I remained where I was every German Archie, field gun, and machine gun within range would try to knock me off the tail on the way down. We were still nearly three miles high and twelve miles over on the German side of the trenches. I decided to climb back in, very carefully digging my knees into the canvas, and gripping the edges of the fuselage. I slowly reached my cockpit. When I had climbed over the gun mounting and had my feet safely on the floor of the cockpit once more, Makepeace turned his head round, stuck his mouth to my ear and yelled `Hedley, what in Hell were you doing out there?'"[7]

Hedley declared, "I was so damned scared I couldn't answer." After successfully landing, Hedley said, "Then some of the other pilots who had seen the incident raced to the side of our ship, shook my hand and told Makepeace that he had a horseshoe observer. Makepeace's eyes nearly popped out of his head. `Blimey, I didn't know I had an angel with me,' was his only comment at the moment."[8]

In a rather typical British understatement, Hedley recorded the January 6 event with the simple flight log book remark: "OP [Offensive Patrol] thrown out of ship Tourcoing 18,000 ft."[9]

No doubt this incredible account first circulated amongst Hedley's peers. In a personal letter in 1927 from a James Allan, formerly of the 20th Squadron, to Hedley he remarked, "Many a time I have told the story to my boys & fellow workmen about your being thrown from your cockpit but never did I think I would see it in print to verify my statements ..."[10] A 1929 book, entitled *Luck Your Silent Partner*, made note of Hedley's extraordinary luck and stated that Lieutenant R. C. Purvis, Recording Officer of the 20 Squadron, had confirmed Hedley's fall and survival by filing the following remark: "January 6, 1918. Mach. No. 7255, Height, 15,000 feet. Lieutenant Makepeace, M. C., reports Captain J. H. Hedley accidentally thrown into air, afterwards alighted on tail same machine and rescued."[11] The story at the time and then related to thousands later, must have generated the reaction "I don't believe that tale." The Hedley story, however, always became the climax and highlight of his numerous lectures.

Hedley later commented that falling out of an open cockpit where there was neither a seat belt nor a parachute was not all that unusual in World War I. He had seen men either fall out or jump out to escape flames to "their doom," he said. What was unique in his case was the landing on the tail of his own aircraft.

The out-of-the-cockpit episode was Hedley's last flight with pilot Makepeace. Makepeace recorded his seventeenth and final aerial victory on January 28, 1918. Later, after being transferred to serve as an instructor at the School of Aerial Fighting and Gunnery at Turnberry, Makepeace and his observer were killed on May 28, 1918, when their F.2B's wings folded up in flight.

Hedley reported that on the same day, January 6, "he made two more flights as a gunner on artillery patrol." When he was asked how he could continue flying after his miraculous survival incident, he replied that he "didn't begin to feel the effects until about two weeks later." "Then he got the jitters," he said. He began to realize that if his plane had been two feet out of line, had side slipped or possibly had continued its dive for any greater distance, he would have been a goner. It's an experience that he does not like to think about, especially when he is flying in an open plane. He told a reporter, "I'm living on borrowed time and how well I know it. It certainly took a lot of whisky and soda to get over that one."[12]

On January 10, Hedley left for England to take a pilot's course at a base near Gloucester. Initially, he received leave to visit Isabella at North Shields prior to beginning his flying training. He then reported to Rendcomb with his first flight of a dual cross country taking place on January 16. After practicing landings and takeoffs, he soloed on January 22nd. He followed this milestone with acrobatics, stunting as he called it, a few days later disaster struck. After barely two weeks in pilot training, he was abruptly ordered back to France as a result of a binge of sixteen officers in pilot training.[13]

Hedley rather delighted in telling what happened when he was back in England. He reported that the officers had reserved stage boxes at the local Vaudeville Show. They made several pub calls before arriving at the theatre and in consequence were quite "well pickled." "Other than they were rather obstreperous and wild in their applause of each act, all went well until an act named 'Craig, Rose and Craig, and Their Half' appeared upon the stage." It was an acrobatic tumbling act, and the "Half" was a midget. They had a large heavy table in the center of the stage and he did hand springs over it.

One of the officers, according to Hedley's story, suggested that the "Half" was bigger than "Scotty" Hedley and the fun began. Reportedly Hedley responded, "Like Hell he is." Immediately, half a dozen officers, including Hedley, piled out of the box, down the stairway, and went to the side of the stage. The midget at this time was on the stage alone walking on his hands and Hedley shouted for him to come off for a minute. The fellow got scared at seeing half a dozen drunken officers in the side wings, shouting at him, and making signs for him to come off. He stood stock still at the far end of the table. With very little urging Hedley walked out on to the stage to measure himself with the dwarf and the little fellow began to run around the table and Hedley ran round after him.

The audience began to shout and cheer. Officers still in boxes began throwing objects on to the stage. They began pelting the orchestra as musicians ran to take cover under the stage. The theatre management had sent for the military police as soon as trouble started and in a few minutes about twenty arrived and escorted all the officers out and took them back to the aerodrome under arrest.

The next morning the officers were all brought before their commanding officer. Hedley became identified as the ring-leader and ordered immediately back to France as an example to the rest. Thus, Hedley's pilot training ended abruptly and not well. He would hence continue his air fighting as an observer.[14]

It is not clear how Hedley managed to get the assignment to pilot training. Certainly, he had plenty of motivation for wanting to become a pilot. The pilot had more prestige in aerial warfare and Hedley had always worried about the possibility that his pilot might become incapacitated leaving him helpless unless he in some way could fly the plane. Nevertheless, no document explains his getting the opportunity of becoming a pilot. Likewise, it is unclear what the pilot training dismissal had on his flying career. He didn't complete the flying training but he eventually would proudly wear pilot wings on his uniform.

In some respects, Captain Hedley's flying training episode seemed to fit with his other recent lucky experiences. Fiery and sometimes boisterous and cantankerous, angering his superiors and other authorities, he always still managed to survive. As in the case of the desperate photo mission, the bizarre accident of falling out of his observer cockpit, and being kicked out of the pilot's course he lived to do another battle and many more battles were on the horizon.

One of Hedley's aerodromes, location unknown, was included in Hedley's papers.

CHAPTER 7

Shot Down

Only a few days after Captain Hedley had his pilot training abruptly terminated and he received orders to return to France, he experienced one of his fiercest aerial battles. On 4 February 1918, Hedley, flying in a Bristol F.2B as an observer with Lt. Thomas Colvill-Jones as pilot,[1] went on an Offensive Patrol with ten other British fighters. At 1055 hours, Hedley's plane attacked a German balloon at map grid 28K5C successfully destroying it. Barely minutes later the entire formation over Roulers encountered and battled twenty-three German scouts. The dog fight, Hedley said, became "one of the biggest scraps twenty squadron ever engaged in."[2] The pilot-observer combination of Hedley-Colvill-Jones claimed the destruction of an Albatros D.V at 1100 hours. Overall, this intense aerial battle produced one of the 20 Squadron's greatest victories with nine German planes and one balloon downed.[3]

Hedley claimed the Wing Commander had been in the air at the time and witnessed the big dog fight. He left early and flew back to the Squadron area to await the return of the fighters. As Hedley's plane arrived, he stood on the field in full flying uniform with Major E. H. Johnston, the Squadron Commander. The Wing Commander and Major Johnston asked Hedley about the furious battle.

Captain Hedley, not identifying the Wing Commander, began cursing the Wing CO for sending them into the air when there were so many Germans on the front. The Squadron Commander tried all sorts of grimaces trying to hush up Hedley but without effect. In desperation he cut in and introduced the Wing Commander to Lt. Colvill-Jones and Captain Hedley.

Speaking directly at Hedley, the Colonel said "Captain Scotty...Oh yes, I remember, met you in England, Captain, two or three weeks ago, didn't I?"

"Yes sir," replied Hedley, as he made a hasty retreat.

Hedley thought the Colonel was a "regular fellow" as he never mentioned a word about the circumstances under which he and Hedley had met at Gloucester. It was the same "gentleman" who had ordered him back to France.[4]

About the same time, adventuresome Captain Hedley became involved in a retaliatory bombing mission. He claimed that German planes never dropped bombs on Allied airfields. The reason for this was not clear but if there was actually any chivalry in the Air Services, which Hedley personally doubted, then maybe this was one case. Regardless, one morning two German planes appeared over the aerodrome and released a couple of bombs. Hedley said "that a couple of eggs were dropped close enough to our hangars and huts to do some damage in both places... making holes in the ground behind our huts large enough to bury a couple of large lorries..."

After this affront, the commanding officer ordered an aircraft that had just taxied back from the gun range to take off and see where the Germans were based. The pilot took off, flew over the trenches, and was able to determine where the German planes landed. The enemy aerodrome was located about a mile northwest of Roulers. Hedley said, "We had a pretty good line on every advanced German airdrome on our section of the Western Front, so it took only a few minutes to decide which field they came from." Retaliation was a foregone conclusion—just one of the rules of the game. "Retaliation was a question of dignity which no self-respecting airman would allow to go unchallenged," alleged Hedley.

In contemplating the retaliatory bomb strike, Hedley noted, "Our supply of bombs consisted of only the small type. Twenty five pound Cooper bombs were all we had, but as each ship could easily carry four of them and we had five ships available, we figured that twenty bombs, if well placed, would at least show the hun that we very much resented having our homes bombed."

In about an hour after the German planes dropped their bombs, five British planes left their field to pay a return visit, "as was socially proper," declared Hedley. Captain Steele, Lieutenants Beaver, Campbell, Makepeace, and

Leigh-Pemberton served as pilots with Hedley as Lt. Campbell's observer. The five Bristol fighters, under Captain Steele's leadership, took off, climbed to seven thousand feet over the airfield, got into formation, and flew toward the lines. It was an unusual procedure for the 20 Squadron planes to cross the trenches at less than 15,000 feet, according to Hedley, and this aroused suspicion of the German anti-aircraft gunners. They welcomed the formation with an unusual quantity of Archies that morning but the planes sailed along unconcernedly. They then nosed down toward the German aerodrome.

Hedley, from his observer's position, reported, "It was really funny to watch the commotion that their approach was causing down below. The Germans on the airdrome could easily be seen running in all directions…" The Bristol fighters circled overhead and dropped their bombs from a height of about 5,000 feet. Some fell on the landing field, others in and around the German hangars and living quarters. The twenty exploding bombs were "quite enough to teach Fritz that the British aviator's home is his castle," declared Hedley.

Except for the anti-aircraft fire, the five plane formation flew unmolested until it approached the trenches on the return trip. There it encountered a flight of the famous Richthofen's circus—eleven triplanes. Hedley said they used to call them "tripes." Remarkably, the ensuing fight was labeled a "mild one." No casualties occurred on either side. The 20 Squadron planes had accomplished their mission and their only object was to get to their own airdrome as soon as possible.

Hedley's aircraft had a narrow escape when two "tripes" dived straight down in front of it and then swinging around climbed vertically shooting upwards underneath. A series of side slips and change of direction every second had saved Hedley's plane. Hedley's pilot performed every maneuver that he knew, all the time trying to sneak away and the Germans trying to head him off and get on his tail. Hedley observed that they were "shooting haphazardly" whether a favorable opportunity presented itself or not. Eventually, pilot Campbell managed to break away and flattened out when British anti-aircraft gunners came to their assistance but not before a burst of lead from one of the German planes passed between Hedley and his pilot, though a space of just inches separated them. The bullets tore a hole big enough to put through a clinched fist. In Hedley's view, "This was simply a run-away fight or a series of run-away fights, although he conceded it probably went down in history in the records of the Red Knight as a complete victory."[5]

Hedley's plane turned northward and flew parallel along the trenches for a short distance headed for home. Hedley, however, noticed two Belgian Spads having a tough time at the guns of three German Fokker planes some two thousand feet below them. Hedley tapped his pilot on the shoulder and pointed to the scrap indicating they should join the fight. Pilot Campbell pushed his stick forward and down they went.

In ten or fifteen seconds they were on top of a Fokker machine with Campbell shooting at one from the front gun at a range of less than fifty yards. Hedley aimed his rear Lewis gun at one of the others and fired several bursts. The Fokkers were taken by surprise and stuck their noses down and beat a hasty retreat eastward with Hedley firing from his rear gun.

The Belgian planes also taken by surprise responded with a roll and loop and flew in circles around the British. They were showing their appreciation for what had happened. One of the Belgian pilots beckoned for them to follow him. Although Campbell and Hedley wanted only to return to base, they decided to see what the Belgian wanted. Presently they dropped down to their aerodrome and the British plane also landed. Upon getting out of their cockpits, the Belgians smothered them with cheek kissing and escorted them to their officers' mess. Campbell and Hedley then received multiple champagne toasts. To their great astonishment, the Belgian commander made a speech and pinned a Belgian Croix de Guerre on their uniforms.

After an hour, Campbell and Hedley jumped back into their planes, took off, and landed at their own airfield. Their commander met them with a scowl as he had worried about their failure to return. When he learned that they had been on what he called a "binge," he raised Hell with both of them and told them that foreign decorations could not be awarded or worn by British aviators except by consent of their wing commander. "And I'll be damned if I recommend them," he concluded. Hedley took off his medal and stuck it in his pocket. Campbell flung his away on the ground. Notification of the awards never appeared in an official Royal Flying Corps communiqué nor in the "Gazette" and the reported medal awards were never recognized.

On 17 February, Hedley flew as an observer with pilot Sergeant Frank Johnson.[6] Frank Johnson, like Makepeace, was an experienced pilot eventually being credited with six enemy planes destroyed and twelve driven out of control. He held a rather unique record as he both piloted and occupied the observer-gunner position, scoring with a combination of different pilots and observers. The Johnson-Hedley flight on the 17th got into another big battle with German aircraft over the area of Moorslede. In the ensuring dog fight, Hedley claimed a Pfalz D.III "driven out of control" at 1120 hours. Just ten minutes later at 1130, Hedley recorded another Pfalz D.III "destroyed." These became victories eight and nine for Captain John Hedley. Pilot Johnson added his ninth and tenth victories. The 20 Squadron would report six enemy aircraft downed in that aerial battle.[7]

Hedley's qualification as a pilot remained unclear as the war went on. He may have lacked a formal designation as such for a considerable time. However, the high attrition of pilots may have eased him into the pilot cockpit. What is clear, nevertheless, is that he told stories of his piloting aircraft. He claimed that he had one pilot experience when he was detailed to a squadron at Bailleul in response to an S.O.S. for pilots. His temporary duty involved flying in a strange squadron and in flying a Sopwith Camel—an aircraft he dreaded and called a "flaming coffin." He never explained how, in short order, he was able to transition to flying the fast, powerful, and highly maneuverable Camel but he delighted in recounting his only battle in one.

"There were five of us on that show and ten miles over on the German side of the fence we encountered a German flight of nine planes. We began to circle round and climb for altitude. The Germans did likewise all the time both flights becoming closer and closer. They had much faster ships than ours and were rapidly gaining height over us. For every hundred feet we rose they seemed to gain two hundred. When they gained an advantage of about a thousand feet they suddenly pushed their noses down and swooped upon us. Two of them were coming straight at me. I flew directly toward them, hoping that a dive at the opportune moment would cause them to overdive me. Then I could swing round and get on one of their tails. They were no amateurs and soon as they went sailing over me and I turned they also turned toward me and zoomed upward as they did so. Gad, those Fokkers could almost climb on their props. They were still above me and held the advantage."

"For a few moments we seemed to be doing nothing but maneuver not a shot was fired. I put my bus through every stunt I could think of in an effort to gain height on them or get on one of their tails. They were both equally determined to get us. Suddenly, I heard the familiar zip-zipzip of machine gun bullets going over my head. The fight was on. In another instant one of their ships sailed directly over the top of my head. Perilously close, his landing gear just cleared my wings. I pulled my stick back with a jerk, throttle full open. My nose went up and I let him have a couple of bursts amidships."

"In my excitement I had failed to realize that the other enemy ship was hanging on my tail, until the thud, thud, of his machine gun bullets spattering my wings brought me to my senses. I flattened out, glanced round, he was directly behind me, less than a hundred yards away, coming straight at me. To dive or climb was out of the question. I could never shake him off as his ship was much faster than mine. Under such circumstances a fellow's brains are in a whirl. He thinks of every conceivable evolution that may or may not get him out of the mess. Like a flash I thought I had heard about but never tried a tactic. I shut my engine as I pulled my nose up. It worked. My ship zoomed up for a moment, then slid backward tail first. The German ship went straight over me. I gave him the gun, dropped my left wing, spiraled, then side slipped from one side to the other until I was down to 5,000 feet. Glanced around again and I was alone."

Captain Hedley thus survived this short flying episode, piloting a Camel no less. He returned to 20 Squadron proclaiming, "I prefer my own squadron, me for the little old Bristol Fighter anytime." Hedley said that the three days with that squadron seemed they were fighting the war alone. "All their flying was done at an altitude below ten thousand feet, where there was much more aerial activity than up aloft in the neighborhood of twenty thousand feet, the habitat of Twenty Squadron."

Hedley did acknowledge that "Bringing down enemy airplanes takes a certain amount of nerve and skillful flying besides a quick use of the gun." He clearly had no desire to be a Camel pilot, however. "One who is in constant dread of the ship he is flying cannot fearlessly engage in air fights. I have seen too many Camels brought down in flames."[8]

The beginning of March 1918 proved deceptively slow for the 20 Squadron air operations. It was probably during this time that athletic Hedley relieved battle and war tension by participating in the sport of soccer. An after the war personal letter to Hedley from a former 20 Squadron member commented, "Perhaps you'll remember me best as 'Jock' Allan. I was goalkeeper for the squadron team. I well remember the games you played at St. Marie Capelle. I think one of the last games you played we were up to the knees in mud & water."[9]

Moving farther into the month of March, however, Squadron activity would abruptly change. The Squadron would become involved in the most furious and climatic aerial operations of the war. A major German offensive had darkly loomed for some time, thought likely to occur in the spring. The British and French were aware of trains arriving loaded with troops coming from the Russian front. The collapse of Tsarist Russia with the resulting Bolshevik Revolution had freed German soldiers for redeployment to the west. This massing of men meant a likely German drive. The questions remained: when and where.

The Germans, on their part, apprehensively weighed the ever increasing numbers of Americans arriving on the Western Front. General Erich von Ludendorff, the lead German commander, decided that a 1918 offensive would begin on the British Somme River sector with the operation code-named "Michael." Ludendorff's plan called for an attack on a forty-to-fifty mile front stretching roughly from Arras on the north to south to the Oise River. His overall strategy sought a breakthrough in this area, driving a wedge between British and French forces, then wheeling into the rear areas eventually pushing the British armies against the Channel ports. This disintegration of the Allied front would lead to a final German victory in the war.

As a part of this ambitious offensive, Ludendorff, as early as June 25, 1917, urged his War Ministry to expand the German air force to better support the ground operations. He proposed increased aircraft and engine production to equip forty new fighter groups and seventeen new flight units. This initiative became known as the American Program with an ultimate goal of at least being equal to the English-French-American air fleet.[10]

Despite the concerted effort by the Germans to conceal their troop concentrations, transporting men and equipment by night, a Royal Flying Corps report provided some intelligence of greater numbers of men and units facing the British front and captured German papers seemed to indicate an early March start date for an offensive. On March 21, 1918, the major German attack began with a massive artillery barrage. The Germans fired 3.2 million rounds on that first day.[11] Explosive and gas shells tended to paralyze and confuse a British response. Behind a creeping artillery barrage, German infantry advanced forcing the British to flee entrenched posts. The British lines fractured and threatened to collapse on that sector of the front.

Heavy fog during the early hours of the offensive prevented British and Allied planes from reconnaissance and ground support. Later the first day weather improved somewhat and British planes attacked the advancing German troopers flying low in order to strafe and bomb. The fluid condition of the battlefield and the uncertain location of British soldiers forced holding fire in some cases. The Royal Flying Corps pressed some thirty-six squadrons into action and flew to the "limit of their ability."[12] They failed to stop German penetration of Allied lines but they did deny German air attacks on British retreating forces. The German squadrons had been concentrated under Manfred von Richthofen and they had prepared advanced airfields, unmanned until the last minute, to avoid revealing offensive preparations. The foggy weather and planned support of the infantry caused low-flying German sorties at first but when the fog lifted frenzied air battles raged between the German aircraft and British planes trying to scout German movements and protect defensive positions.

Hedley and the 20 Squadron plunged into this whirlwind of air activity. Emphasis by necessity, went to strafing and bombing German troops and transports. Although atrocious flying weather hampered all operations, British air crews bravely took to the skies to support the beleaguered infantry. The German Jastas tried to prevent reconnaissance and attacks on their advancing soldiers. Fierce dog fights developed with heavy losses on both sides.

On March 23, shortly after noon (12:10 P.M.), Hedley, flying as an observer with Captain Robert K. Kirkman in Bristol Fighter B1156, had a successful engagement with German Albatros Scouts. Captain Kirkman from Cosby, Leicestershire, the eighth child of a farmer, had started military service as a private in an artillery company. He was appointed a flying officer on February 14, 1917, and became a flight commander with 20 Squadron on December 18, 1917. He would total three Albatros D.Vs as destroyed and five driven down out of control and receive the Military Cross. Thus, Kirkman, like other pilots that Hedley teamed with, was a veteran warrior.

Their March 23rd "Combats in the Air" narrative read as follows:

"Whilst on Offensive Patrol, 10 Bristol Fighters encountered 7 Albatros Scouts E. of WERVICQ. B1156 dived on one of the E. A. and the pilot (Capt. R. K. Kirkman, M.C.) fired about 100 rounds into it at about 100 yds. range. The E. A. went down in a vertical nose dive and shortly after, volumes of smoke were observed to be issuing from the enemy machine which continued to go down, apparently on fire."

"About 12:45 p. m. 10 Albatros Scouts were engaged E. of MENIN. B1156 dived on one of the E. A. and, after the pilot fired about 100 rounds into it, the

E. A. went down in a spin. The Observer Capt. Hedley fired one drum into it as it went down. The E. A. was observed to pull out of the spin but went down immediately afterwards out of control. The latter E. A. is confirmed by Corpl. Mather, Observer in machine No. B1122." This action reportedly took place at 14,000-17,000 feet altitude.[13]

Hedley's success in the 23 March aerial battle increased his total for enemy downed aircraft to ten and eleven. Little did he know at that time, these would be his last.

There has been some difficulty in reconciling all of Hedley's victories, as well as those of other pilots-observers, with the reported German losses. In the midst of heated battles with imperfect verification there were individual claims that did not always match the enemy's record. Nevertheless, these were the official numbers that Hedley could proudly report.

Hedley's observer skills and battle successes to this point earned him the award of the French Croix de Guerre, recorded on April 28, 1918. The simple citation stated that Captain John Herbert Hedley distinguished himself on 6 November, 1917, as an observer in the destruction of enemy aircraft and a balloon.[14] Hedley did not see the French citation and medal until his return to England after the war ended. The French reference to destruction of a balloon prompted Hedley to say that one balloon was enough to cure him of ever trying to get another. "They were so well protected by anti-aircraft gunners that it was almost suicide to dive on them," he said. "I still don't know how we got the one I did without being shot down. Our plane was riddled."[15] This opinion was shared by most World War I aviators.

On March 26, five days into the German offensive, the weather turned cold and clear and air operations even increased. Major General Salmond, Commander of the Royal Flying Corps in France, ordered, "Bomb and shoot up everything that can be seen. Very low flying necessary, all risks to be taken. Urgent."[16] Despite its all-out effort, the RFC bombing and strafing caused German casualties but failed to stop the German advance. Enemy troops drove some forty miles into the British sector and the RFC sustained heavy losses in the low flying over the battlefield. By April 4, however, the front began to stabilize due to French reserves plugging gaps in the line and the Germans outrunning their logistical support.

In the initial period of the German offensive the 20 Squadron and Captain Hedley became involved in another repercussion of the massive attack—the need to withdraw from some forward aerodromes. An advanced airfield near Ypres became endangered by pressing German infantry and the squadron commander there decided he would have to abandon the airbase and move farther west. He had more aircraft than pilots and sent an urgent request to 20 Squadron for five men to fly the ships away.

Although it is unclear whether Hedley had fully attained his pilot rating, he and four other 20th pilots reported for duty to ferry the aircraft. "When we arrived at the airdrome and reported to the commanding officer, he instructed us to go into the officer's mess and standby. That meant we were not to divest ourselves of any of our flying clothes," said Hedley.[17]

The commanding officer came rushing into where Hedley and company were waiting; and according to Captain "Scotty," he looked over the group, including three new pilot arrivals, and asked, "Can any one of you fellows pray?"

The rescue pilots looked at each other and then one innocently answered "Yes sir, I can."

The commanding officer said, "Then get right down on your knees and pray. The Germans are right here on us, the rest of you dash to the airdrome, get into the ships and beat it. We are one ship short."[18]

The emergency evacuation apparently succeeded with Hedley as a pilot.

Twenty Squadron received orders to abandon its missions of photography and fighting at high altitudes over the Ypres front and to concentrate on road strafing on the Somme sector. Due to the precarious situation, each Bristol carried eight twenty-five pound Cooper bombs fixed in racks under the wings. The new sorties were directed at bombing the advancing enemy columns. The Squadron still based at St. Marie Capelle would utilize an advanced airfield at Bray, where after arriving at daybreak, planes would operate from there until dusk and then return to the main base. The crews were making as many as four shows a day. Late in March, the 20th would return to its old aerodrome at Boisdinghem.[19]

Hedley had been assigned to low-level bombing and machine gunning of enemy troops on the Bapaume-Albert road section. He reported that the weather all the preceding week had been "deplorable." "It rained incessantly. Thick mizzly rain like wet fog. The clouds were black and very low. It remained almost as dark as night all day long." Hedley said that the Germans couldn't have had better weather for their purpose if they had made it themselves.

On March 27, Captain "Scotty" Hedley, upon returning from each of his first two morning shows, reported Albert was still in British possession. After his third show, however, the Germans had entered that location. "They were making alarming progress," Hedley said.[20]

In these hectic days of the German offensive, Hedley expressed his admiration and respect for 20 Squadron Commander, Major E. H. Johnston. Hedley said the Major made a practice of coming up to every ship and shaking hands with each crewman before every show, with a "real honest to God handshake."

Johnston invariably shouted, "God protect you and bring you safely back again old boy."

Hedley added, "Sometimes I fancied there were tears in his eyes as each show was a period of agonizing suspense ... until we got safely back again."[21]

Hedley noted an unusual event on March 27. He thought it was a "strange coincidence" that the gunnery officer's large German police dog came running up to his aircraft at the aerodrome just before he took off. "Scotty" was fond of the dog and it followed him about but it had never before jumped and barked near his cockpit. Sergeant James Allan came running and had to drag the dog away before the take-off.[22]

About half past three in the afternoon, Captain Robert Kirkman, pilot, and Captain John Hedley, observer, in Bristol F.2B (B1156), left the aerodrome for the fourth time that day and made straight for Albert.[23] There were so many aircraft concentrating on the Bapaume road that they flew on to Peronne. Hedley thought the visibility was so bad that they could hardly see half a mile ahead so they went low to 200 feet. Then dropping to 100 feet, they flew over the heads of the enemy troops. Hedley observed the German infantry was "marching along the roads in regular textbook formation, columns of fours with their transport and guns behind them." As Hedley and Kirkman drew closer, they were welcomed with machine gun fire, flaming onions, and shells from the numerous German light field guns. Then they dropped the eight bombs one by one, scattering the Germans to the sides of the road.

The Kirkman-Hedley crew was performing the typical bombing and strafing attack used by the Bristol Fighters. It began with a rapid dive to the target, followed by the release of the twenty-five pound bomb, and with the climb back to altitude the observer would rake the enemy with machine gun fire from his rear Lewis gun. This tactic would be repeated until gasoline or ammunition ran out.[24]

"Having disposed of the bombs we turned around and dove down on them, attacking them with machine gun bullets all the way, going down in a mad frenzy until we got so close to those German troops that propeller blades would almost tear away the steel helmets," declared Hedley. "Then he would suddenly 'yank her up,' leaving me almost standing on my head." Hedley said that this seemed to offer him "… my share of the fun where momentum, gravitation, and various other forces work miracles in the air and one forgets all about the probability of falling out of the machine."[25] Despite Hedley's strong feelings that the war's so called chivalry was bunk and there was nothing but horror, he said, "There was something strangely fascinating about that job of diving, riddling, raking that human target a few feet below with machine gun bullets."[26]

Over Faucaucourt, disaster was about to strike, however. Hedley stated, "On this occasion we had wandered rather too far over the line and found ourselves alone, owing to the fact that the country was entirely new to us and in the excitement we had lost all sense of direction."[27] At about 3:30, having dropped the bombs and depleted their ammunition, Captain Hedley and Captain Kirkman headed for home. To their surprise, an Albatros Scout dove through the clouds on to their tail. "I suddenly felt the vibration of machine gun bullets hitting my own machine," remembered Hedley. "I looked around to see what it was all about and there was that great red machine twenty or thirty yards behind us, both his machine guns spitting fire. We pulled the nose of our machine up so as to hide in the clouds. As we climbed I noticed a cold numbing sensation starting at my toes and gradually creeping up my legs toward my waist. I thought my legs had been shot through but afterwards discovered that both gasoline tanks had been riddled and it was the gasoline soaking up my flying shoes which had caused the ice cold numbing sensation."

"Then our propeller began to sputter and stopped. I glanced around to see if an enemy plane was still around and to my horror saw a cloud of black smoke and flames leaping up from the plane ten or twelve feet into the air. I had witnessed many ships brought down in flames during my period in France and I dreaded that more than anything else. I believe I got the greatest scare of my life. The thing which I had dreaded most had come to pass. The ship was on fire. The engine had stopped. We were up about a couple of hundred feet. There was only one way to get down safely and that was to side slip. We side slipped almost to the ground, swang the nose round, and landed on a roadway. I got clear of the ship, ran over into a ditch, and when the ship had all burned up, German soldiers came running up to me with fixed bayonets, shouting as loud as they could, Englander, Swinehunt, and a lot more stuff I couldn't understand. I was almost frantic, cursing my bad luck, laughing, shouting, crying I know not what. Then everything became dark and when I came back to my senses a big German officer was standing alongside me with six soldiers."[28]

Captain John Hedley in this dark moment might have cursed his "bad luck" but in many ways his phenomenal good luck had occurred again. He had survived being shot down. Despite his great fear of dying in a flaming aircraft, he had escaped the flames of his Bristol Fighter. He was physically intact—able to run to a nearby ditch. His pilot had also survived without serious injury. He had been made a prisoner of war but with the heighten tensions of the battlefield he was lucky he had not been shot on the spot by the angry German troopers. Indeed, "Scotty" Hedley seemed to further merit the title of "The Luckiest Man Alive."

For many years, Hedley and others believed that he and Kirkman had been shot down by Manfred von Richthofen himself flying in his bright red Fokker Tr. 1. Hedley long, and rather proudly, claimed this was the case. Later research, however, established that it was Leutnant Karl Gallwitz of Jasta 2 that shot down the Hedley plane. Gallwitz would become a German double ace with ten aerial victories. After beginning flying on the Russian front, he joined Jasta Boelcke, and in the latter part of 1917, downed British ace Arthur Rhys-Davids. In 1918, he would score five victories including shooting down Kirkman-Hedley. Gallwitz later crashed but survived after his tenth claim on April 21, 1918.[29] Regardless of the identity of the German adversary, Captain Hedley and Captain Kirkman were now German prisoners and their aerial fighting was over.

While Captain Hedley and Captain Kirkman would no longer be a part of 20 Squadron operations, that unit continued the fight to the end of the war. It would eventually claim 613 air combat victories with 315 of that total listed as aircraft destroyed. This record made the Squadron a "top scoring unit" in World War I aerial warfare. Authors Norman Franks and Frank Bailey pointed to the teamwork of the Bristol pilot and gunner as the major reason for the success of 20 Squadron, terming the pilot-gunner team "the finest fighting combination of the air war."[30] Captain John Hedley's role as a 20 Squadron observer, with credit for downing ten German aircraft and one balloon, perhaps did not make him a major contributor to the large 20 Squadron total victories.[31] Nevertheless, his record in World War I aerial combat, occurring in a relatively short but climatic period, highlighted the importance of the observer and established his key personal characteristics of courage, persistence, and mission dedication.

This photograph of primarily 20 Squadron enlisted men, dated 13 November 1918, was included in Hedley's collection of war items. He was a prisoner of war at this time.

GD9888   500   8/17   HWV(P)   H956
W6075—HP1954   1000   3/18

Please direct reply to—
The Military Secretary,
14, Albemarle Street,
London, W.1.

WAR OFFICE,

FOREIGN DECORATIONS SECTIONS (M.S. 3B),

14, ALBEMARLE STREET,

LONDON, W.1.

October 21st 1918.

Madam,

I am directed to send you herewith, by registered package, the
Croix de Guerre   the award of which to
Captain J.H.HEDLEY R.A.F.

appeared in the *London Gazette* of _____ 17.8.18.

I am to ask that you will kindly complete the attached
form of receipt for the decoration in question, and that it may be
returned to the above address as soon as possible.

I am,   Madam,

Your obedient Servant,

[signature] Major,

for Military Secretary.

To   Mrs J.HEDLEY
     10 Chirton West View
           North Shields

While Hedley was a prisoner of war, this document forwarded notification of the award of the French Croix de Guerre to Mrs. Hedley on October 21, 1918.

CHAPTER 8

Prisoner of War

From the very beginning of the big German offensive, the 20 Squadron had conducted four shows a day, four times over the heads of the German soldiers, dropping bombs in their midst and raking them with machine gun fire at point-blank range. Four times a day, between dawn and sunset, the planes took off on their dangerous missions. In the midst of all this, Hedley somehow found time to write the following to wife Isabella on the very day he was posted as missing:

"This horrid business is like a nightmare, but through it all I often see the sun shining in the heavens and the smile of the most adorable little girl in the world. I cannot tell you darling how much I love you, there are not sufficient adjectives in the English language. But if I die, though I don't think I shall, you may rest assured sweetheart that I shall have died extremely happy with thoughts of you."[1]

In great contrast to these affectionate lines, Hedley somehow and some-time later, claimed he penned these thoughts:

"God, how utterly miserable I am. I have cried and cried like a wee baby, but what the Hell's the use. I am a prisoner of war, doomed to a living death for God knows how long. Life? Well, what is life anyway? Not worth a damn cent in this bloody war. I go down on my knees and curse, and curse. God, why in Hell's name don't you let them kill me. I hate everything. I hate every-body. I hate myself. This is Hell. God, I'm going crazy. I am going crazy."[2]

No doubt Captain Hedley quickly realized his terrible fate. His flying was ended and he faced being a prisoner of war for as long as the war lasted. He had always seemed sensitive to the horrors and injustices he saw in the war. So his initial cry of "going crazy" would surely be repeated during the months of confinement ahead. Hedley, like many other prisoners, would find the mental strain probably worse than the physical abuse.

Hedley apparently did not have much time to reflect on his lucky and amazing survival of a crash following being shot down. Pilot Captain Kirkman also surprisingly had escaped injury. Both Kirkman and Hedley ran away from their downed plane to the side of a nearby ditch and were each surrounded by German soldiers. From that point the two officers experienced the prisoner of war ordeal together.

Very soon after his capture, Hedley began making diary-type remarks in a small pocket-size "Notiz-Buch" that he must have obtained some way from the Germans. In his "Wed 27 Mar 1918" entry, the day he was shot down, he scribbled the following diary comment. "When brought down my clothes were saturated with petrol and I was soaked through to the skin up to the waist. Found two bullet holes through my left boot and one through Kirkman's dress cap which was in the machine under my seat."[3] Hedley added, "The Germans refused to allow us to get our tins of emergency rations from the machine...The machine burned up." The German officer, who approached the disconsolate Hedley, informed him that he was lucky he had been nearby when he came down, as the soldiers would surely have killed him for dropping bombs on them. He added that he had orders to take as many prisoners as he could or even he would have had no compassion and would have let his soldiers finish him off.

Hedley and Kirkman were stripped of their flying clothes leaving them with just the uniforms they were wearing and their flight boots. The Germans took valuables such as watches, cigarette cases, and French money and then began a "pilgrimage which lasted several weeks." Three German soldiers were placed in charge of Hedley and Kirkman and they spoke neither French nor English and with Hedley and Kirkman's lack of German proficiency, they claimed they had "one Hell of a time." They determined that no one seemed to know what to do with them so they tramped about in circles over the recent battlefield.

Hedley said, "The ground was strewn with dead no matter which way we turned. Every here and there groups of three or four British Tommies lay where they had fallen with a shattered machine gun in their midst, all that was left to tell a tale of a grim struggle to the bitter end. Others had dropped as they ran. Some of their faces bore unmistakable expressions of horror and anguish and some just a sickly smile. The whole thing was hideous. War is Hell let loose."[4]

At one point in the prisoner march, Hedley recorded watching an aerial battle with Richthofen's circus attacking a British R E. 8, which he considered one of the slowest and least maneuverable of planes. The surely doomed R E. 8 was saved by the sudden appearance of five British S. E. 5 scout machines with the Germans breaking off the attack.[5]

Hedley continually complained about the lack of food provided by his captors. On Thursday, 28 March, he said, "At 8 AM the German soldiers gave us a piece of dry bread and some hot coffee." Hedley in another writing stated he had desperately scavenged any edibles from the bodies of the dead Tommies. As the prisoner march continued, Hedley commented, "Arrived here about 6 PM. We had now 30 English soldiers with us. We were given some hot herb tea at 7 PM and at 9 PM some cabbage & potato soup. We slept all night in a barn which we found very cold…"[6]

On Friday, 29 March 1918, Hedley recorded, "We were given one loaf to each five prisoners and a basin of hot tea and left Ronsay at 8 am for LeCateau arriving at the latter place about 11:30 am. On arrival there we were taken to a large weaving factory where we stayed a few days. The Germans were breaking up all the machinery in the place…At tea time everyone was given a green postcard to fill up with Rank, Name & Regt. which the German NCO in charge said would take 5 days to reach the W.O. [War Office] in London."[7] Perhaps this was some comfort to Hedley as it would let Isabella know he was still alive. Isabella had received a hand-written letter from 20 Squadron's Major Johnston informing her that her husband's plane had failed to return. He offered "that no news is good news in this instance."[8]

On April 1, Hedley wrote in his diary that he left LeCateau by train for Karlsruhe. He noted several station stops where he always recorded the meager food provided and complained that the Germans charged them outrageous prices for everything. At one stop he reported "…We pooled our money — five in our carriage — and had a table spoonful of boiled potatoes cold, done up with vinegar." Hedley's train passed on through Karlsruhe and arrived at Rastatt on April 3rd. The prisoners were marched to a prison and ushered into a hut with about eighty beds in it. For the next several days, complaints continued about the meals but one day postcards were sold and the men were allowed to send one home. "Everyone seems to have a sort of tired feeling," Hedley said. "Hardly enough energy to go for meals. Managed to get a book to read today."[9]

Hedley stated that on April 10 "senior officers in each hut complained of food shortage." The reply was not unexpected. "The commandant said we were getting the same as German officers. That the country was very short of all kinds of food and other things." In fact, Hedley was gaining interesting intelligence from the Germans. In an early diary entry he wrote, "All the German soldiers think the war will be over in two or three weeks. One English speaking NCO said Germany couldn't possibly hang out over six months owing to internal conditions, food, clothing, etc."[10]

At LeCateau Hedley and Kirkman underwent prisoner interrogation by a "Colonel of the German Flying Corps" but the questioning did not begin well. A German guard ushered Hedley into a room with nothing in it except a wooden table and a couple of wooden benches. A lighting fixture hung from the center of the ceiling. When the escort left, Hedley alone, climbed upon the table and began examining the fixture to see if it contained a secret microphone. He was caught in the act when two German officers stepped into the room. One officer sarcastically asked if Captain Hedley had lost something to which Hedley replied, "Yes sir, my liberty." The officer snarled at him. Hedley declared, "I got in bad right at the start." He also concluded that "not one of the Germans, had any sense of humor." He was reminded that his future happiness as a prisoner of war would depend upon the accuracy and completeness with which he answered the questions that were put to him.[11]

The other officer began questioning. Hedley recalled that the man was tall and thin and wore a perpetual frown. His hair was cut close and he had a heavy mustache and a goatee. Hedley declared he looked like a baboon. "As I sat gazing at him I kept thinking if the Lord didn't intend us to laugh why did he ever create a monkey?" The feisty prisoner Hedley plunged into deeper trouble when he was asked where he was born and he replied England. "What part?" the officer asked, and Hedley snapped, "All of me." With this rejoinder, the officer reached across the table and socked Hedley on the jaw. Hedley said that he then refused to talk and the officer became furious. He called for the guard and turned to Hedley and said, "You bloody English mule, you will be taken out into a field where you can eat grass for twenty four hours."[12]

The German guard, as ordered, took Hedley to a field, tied a rope around his waist, and tied the end to a stake. For twenty four hours he was kept there with a sentry watching over him. Hedley said that he tried to sleep but with being weary, cold, foot sore, and overall tired of life, he did not rest.

After wandering around the battlefield for two or three weeks, and after passing through LeCateau, Hedley was taken to a detention camp at Rastatt on the Rhine and placed amongst Russian prisoners. Hedley thought it strange that the Germans were still holding numbers of Russians after their capitulation so many months ago. He still had to scrounge for food and reported he was inoculated eight times — for what purpose he could never determine. He believed the inoculations along with lack of food caused a rapid deterioration in his physical condition. After five weeks, he claimed he was so weak he could hardly stand erect. In addition, pronounced feelings of depression would hit him during the day.[13]

Hedley made a diary entry on April 13, saying, "Kirkman, Pope 2/Lt, Redpath Lt and myself made a written application to the Commandant asking to be removed to a proper R.F.C. officers' camp as soon as possible as we are the only R.F.C. officers in this block." He also noted times when he was paid German marks which in some cases were quickly re-collected as a payment for food and articles.

Later in that same week, Thursday, 18 April, Hedley declared it was a "Red letter day." He had gotten a piece of sausage for breakfast and dried fruit stewed, and coffee at 4 PM. Even the soup at midday was above average, he said. His entry for that day also reported that a "series of lectures and debates have been arranged by officers in his block." An interesting debate ensued on whether it was practicable or desirable to settle international disputes by arbitration or war. The next day, there was a lecture on Tea and Rubber plantations.[14] Hedley and his fellow prisoners were already seeking ways to fill their time and ease the oppressive boredom.

On 26 April, almost a month after being shot down and taken prisoner, Hedley left Rastatt and arrived at Karlsruhe. He was marched to some huts and was questioned again. Several days later, he left by train for Landshut where Hedley and others were taken to a compound. "We were stripped of all clothing in fact everything & given prison clothing as worn by the Russian prisoner." Prisoners were confined to huts, but on 8 May, Hedley said that his clothing had been returned except for his flying boots. He also received food from the Swiss Red Cross. Eventually, after almost three months, he arrived at the flying officers' camp at Holzminden on the Weser and he received the designation of "No. 1237 Hauptman Scotty."

A military band escorted the prisoners from the train depot to the Holzminden barracks, playing enroute "The Watch on the Rhine." Into the camp, the prisoners were stripped naked while guards examined them and their clothes for any hidden map or compass. Hedley said, "They made their examination as embarrassing as they possibly could." Holzminden had two large, four story, pre-war infantry barracks built of concrete with corridors running the full length of the building and rooms leading directly off the halls. Hedley was assigned to Room 84. It was about thirty-six feet long and twenty-four feet wide.

Holzminden, far to the east from the Western Front, on the Weser River in Lower Saxony, had been an army barracks constructed in 1913. It became a more secure camp for allegedly rebellious World War I prisoners and quickly became known as one of the most notorious German prisoner of war encampments. It opened in September 1917 with the several buildings housing 550 officers and up to 100 orderlies. Its World War I notorious reputation stemmed largely from its Commandant, Hauptman Charles Niemeyer.

On "Hauptman Scotty's" second day at Holzminden, the camp Commandant introduced himself. He was Captain Charlie Niemeyer, who had left his home in Milwaukee, Wisconsin, two months before the war began to rejoin the German army. He became known as "Milwaukee Bill." The temperamental Niemeyer quickly made it clear that he hated the English. He set strict controls and brutally treated the prisoners with contempt. He liberally employed solitary confinement, particularly for escape attempts, withheld food rations, looted Red Cross packages, and verbally harangued the prisoners. Reportedly, his own guards hated him. Hedley asserted, "He was one of the most inhuman wretches I ever met in my life, and I'm not saying this simply because he was German."[15]

In front of the barracks there was space, called a spielplatz, used for exercising. Niemeyer walked the area every day. Hedley alleged that when he encountered the Commandant he would say, "Good morning Hauptman Scotty" to which he would reply, "Good morning Hauptman Niemeyer," whereupon the Commandant would spit in his face. "That sort of treatment went on constantly, and nearly drove us crazy to control ourselves under such provoking circumstances." Hedley's hatred of Niemeyer continued long after his eventual release. He claimed that he intended to go to Milwaukee and kill him whenever he went to the United States.[16]

British officer H. G. Durnford, in his personal account of his Holzminden imprisonment, also reported on Niemeyer's rants against the British. For example, in response to any violations of a regulation prohibiting hanging of laundry on a line, Durnford said that Niemeyer would find amusement in making "fierce onslaughts with his stick on the washing hanging out to dry on the wire fence between the two main buildings. He would lunge at some unoffending undergarment, spit it, brandish it violently in the air, and then trample on it."[17]

After being incarcerated at Holzminden, Hedley's diary entries became sporadic and almost one liners —mere brief bullets of information. He took note, for example, of Kirkman's birthday (28) on June 25 and recorded dates when individuals went to solitary confinement which he called the "Jug."

He did write that on the night of July 23 and 24, "Twenty nine officers escaped by tunnel from 'B' House."[18] Sixty prisoners from "B" House (Hedley was in "A" House) had dug a tunnel over many months that led from the foundation to some fifty yards into a field of rye outside the prison walls. The prisoners had started the tunnel in November 1917, they painstakingly worked in three-man teams, in three-hour shifts, using small trowel like tools. The excavated earth moved by a basin and pulley system and was deposited on a cellar roof. On the appointed day, the officers made their way through the tunnel from midnight to 5:00 A.M. carefully staging their departures at ten minute intervals. Unfortunately, the tunnel collapsed after the 29th man closing the escape route. The prison escape had been aided by three German camp members who supplied items like torches and information. Ten officers successfully made it to neutral borders but nineteen, scattered over the countryside, were captured and returned to camp to face solitary confinement and other punishment.[19]

As might be expected, the tunnel escape infuriated Commandant Niemeyer. H. G. Durnford remarked that "for several days he achieved a crescendo of fury and malevolence and maintained all the outward characteristics of a mad bull."[20] Hedley, Durnford, and others concluded, rather joyfully, that Niemeyer, reported at age sixty-two, was "looking every day of it." Niemeyer had complained that British officers were making him an old man before his time.[21]

All the compound experienced the repercussions of the escape. Hedley wrote, "Baths closed, tin room & parcel room closed, walk stopped. Officers forbidden to go into any other room but their own, or into the other House."[22] Hedley indicated that walks did not resume until August.

Hedley maintained that the prisoners survived on food sent by the British and Swiss Red Cross. Even then some parcels of food, tobacco, and cigarettes reportedly were sent but mysteriously ended up "lost in transit."[23] It seemed that food problems persisted forever for the Holzminden prisoners. Commandant Niemeyer's "camp orders" stated, "The daily meals consist of a sufficient quantity in accordance with the circumstances of war." Food or not, breakfast began at 8:30 with a midday meal noon to 12:30, tea at 4 P.M., and supper at 6:15 to 7 P.M. in a dining hall.[24]

All officers had to be up and dressed by 7 A.M. with lights out by 10 P.M. Officers, by camp rules, had to remain undressed in their beds from 10 P.M. to 7 A.M. Then there were roll calls at 9 A.M. and 5 P.M. with officers properly dressed. This constituted Hedley and Kirkman's regimented, invariable, daily routine. After the escape, rules and routines were more strictly enforced.[25]

In addition to his small diary, Hedley kept a nine by six inch, clothbound, sketch book in which he did some finely crafted pen and ink drawings (some enhanced with color) depicting various prison scenes. On the cover he wrote, "Capt. J. H. Hedley RFC, Prisoner of War, March 27th 1918 to Dec. 14th 1918," but the contents included only his time at Holzminden. Within the book were photographs of some of the officer staged drama productions. There were obviously rudimentary sets but rather elaborate costuming, especially for female characters. One has to wonder how such costumes were obtained. Durnford in his book on the tunnel escape indicated that costumes were obtained from nearby communities, probably openly purchased. There were certain restrictions, however, on theatrical wardrobes. Male and female parts were kept strictly apart under lock and key and under the supervision of a particular British officer. "It had always been a strict injunction of ever successive senior British officer that on no account was there to be any tampering with these clothes for purposes of escape." The reason was clear. "It was necessary in the interests of that large section of the community which relied on the periodical 'shows' — whether as performers or spectators — for their principal means of relief from the enui of prison existence."[26] Hedley did several pen drawings of his performance in "Pygmalion" and with a tall officer doing what he labeled as "simultaneous dancing." The latter he dated as 13 October.[27]

Hedley tried keeping his mind alert by writing articles in notebooks on subjects such as money and the Spanish Plague. On occasion, he dabbled in writing poetry and attending officer-led lectures on military law and military tactics. In his diary, he said he "commenced to learn violin —1st lesson on August 9." A second lesson occurred on the 15th and a third on the seventeenth.[28]

Despite this evidence of varied activity, Hedley took special note of what he called "The Psychology of Prisoners of War." He copied, in beautiful handwriting, portions of an article entitled "Barbedwireitis." He clearly believed the words explained and described the mental state of Holzminden prisoners. He offered that men living together in the close quarters of a camp soon brought on an "aversion for one's comrades."[29] Hedley thought that the mental stress led to selfishness and odd behavior. He, himself, stated he spent time collecting pieces of old clothing, torn shirts, pants, and whatever, for the sole purpose of making a parachute to be able to jump out of the fourth floor window and escape.[30] He said that the "lack of individual privacy and solitude becomes a torture." In time, the prison experience caused a decline in all individual interests rendering men as more zombie-like creatures. Hedley agreed with a summary comment that "for the prisoner of war there is always the 'want to and can't'!"[31]

Holzminden prisoners had high hopes of immediate release with the news of the Armistice on 11 November 1918 but these hopes were quickly dashed. With the political turmoil in Germany at the end of the war, Hedley said that the German officers fled the camp and enlisted men took over command. The enlisted men were now members of the Soldadenrat, the Soldier's Council. Hedley painted a highly unfavorable picture of prolonged negotiations between prisoner leaders and the Soldadenrat. In desperation, according to Hedley, the entire prisoner population of British officers, approximately 700, decided to set fire to the camp. "So at a previously arranged hour and night, every one of us filed out of the two barracks carrying one or two pieces of wooden furniture. We piled it up alongside the walls of 'A' House and set fire to it. In a few minutes the sky was red as the dry wood blazed away."[32] Holzminden lay in a bowl shaped valley and German police dogs patrolled outside the prison at night. With the fire, dogs howled and barked, church bells pealed in villages, and fire alarms went off all around. Hoses brought out to fight the flames were cut by the officers. With so many prisoners against some fifty armed Germans, the guards feared a riot and began to negotiate for the prisoner release. The prisoner demand for unconditional, immediate release was met and the prisoners helped putting out the fire.

The next morning the officers walked out of Holzminden to the depot where a couple of freight trains were waiting. Hedley said that the men were "Hysterical with excitement, we laughed, we wept, we shouted, we moaned and wept again, and again, and again."[33] They went straight to Holland. Hedley travelled from Rotterdam to the port of Hull on England's east coast.[34] Hedley's service record indicated that he was "Repatriated" (the British Government term) on December 13,1918.[35] He arrived in England on December 14 and this was the date he considered the true end of his prisoner status. Isabella met him at nearby Grimsby.[36] He was home at last only a few days before Christmas 1918.

Several days after arriving in England, Hedley and others received a letter of welcome home from King George V. It began, "The Queen joins me in welcoming you on your release from the miseries and hardships, which you have endured with so much patience and courage."[37] While Hedley appreciated the King's letter, he could feel that no one could truly understand the mental and physical anguish he endured as a prisoner of war. He had been changed by his months of confinement. He was no longer the cocky young man of his early military days. Furthermore, like most returning veterans, he indeed was ready to put his military service behind him and start anew.

Some months later after Hedley had returned to England he met a Standing Committee of Enquiry composed of high ranking officers who examined the circumstances of his becoming a prisoner of war. Hedley was cleared of any misdeeds. The War Office statement, dated 25 July 1919 read: "The Secretary of the War Office presents his compliments to Captain J. H. Hedley, Royal Air Force, and begs to state that he is commanded by the Army Council to inform him that his statement regarding the circumstances of his capture by the enemy having been investigated, the Council considers that no blame attaches to him in the matter."[38] With this action, Hedley officially ended his British military service.

A grim Captain Hedley, seated in the center, poses with a group of fellow officer prisoners of war at Karlsruhe, Germany, on April 30, 1918. This photograph became a postcard and was sent to Hedley's wife at North Shields. Hedley wrote: "Still keeping quite well. Fondest love, from Herbert."

German Captain "Charlie" Niemeyer with a handwritten note at the bottom calling him "The Holzminden Bully."

This scene of a Holzminden POW theater production, entitled "Home John," captures one way prisoners sought to relieve camp boredom.

POW barracks at Holzminden Camp in Germany

This snapshot was contained in Hedley's prisoner of war materials. Since it indicated the time of 1917-19, it may have been one of his last photographs as an active duty RFC/RAF officer.

CHAPTER 9

To America

Captain John Hedley's arrival at Hull, England, on December 14, 1918, must have been a joyous occasion. He was truly free at last. He was home and Isabella would be meeting him. Following setting foot on England's soil, he received about eight weeks leave during which time he had some medical attention. Records state, however, that his RAF pay would end on February 27, 1919.[1] This would indicate that his discharge from the RAF occurred at that time.

Isabella met "Scotty" at Grimsby. It is not clear why the happy meeting occurred there rather than at the home in North Shields. Furthermore, apparently John, Isabella, and John Jr. remained in this community, as a second son, Sidney Roland, was born at Grimsby on December 16, 1919.

Hedley sought to return to his pre-war career as an accountant but he offered little description of his life and work following his release from the British military. He served as an auditor with the Newcastle firm Monkhouse, Goddard, Price Waterhouse from April 1919 to September 1920.[2] His actual work may have been in the Grimsby area as the family continued to live at that port city.

At the beginning of the fall of 1920, he made a momentous decision to terminate his employment in England and to seek a new life in the United States. The idea of immigrating to the United States probably had been planted long ago by his father who reportedly saw more opportunity there.[3]

Nevertheless, the rather abrupt decision to go to America, leaving Isabella with toddler son Sidney Roland, contained many unanswered questions. Regardless, after a relatively short time back in England, where he grew to manhood, the restless John Hedley seemed determined to be on the move again.

John H. Hedley set sail for America on October 21, 1920, travelling on the Red Star Steamship Line *Finland* from Southampton to New York, arriving there on October thirty-first. He travelled alone leaving Isabella and the two children in England. He wrote that he made this choice: "For no other reason than that of seeking greater opportunities in life."[4]

Hedley spent a few days in New York City and then boarded a train for Chicago arriving there on November 5, 1920. "I had no particular reason for coming to Chicago, although my friends say that it was the only place in the world where I could feel quite at home after the war," he said.[5] He looked for work as an accountant and obtained quick employment. He served as a Certified Public Accountant for Chicago firm Marwick Mitchell from November 1920 to September 1921. He moved to Galva, Illinois, to work as an accountant for Hayes Pump and Planter Company from September 1921 to July 1922.[6] He then returned to Chicago and began a more extensive job as an auditor. Very soon after arriving in Chicago, he received an assignment to do an audit in Indianapolis. Such travel suddenly broadened his introduction to the United States. He declared that it brought him into "contact with a bunch of real Americans" and they "had a great time." He added, "I hadn't yet learned of prohibition." His public accountant work and particularly auditing led to trips to other states and after only a few months he had audit business in Pittsburgh and Cleveland. Hedley reported that he found "established English colonies" in other locations. "Some of the Englishmen I met thought I was becoming Americanized too quickly and tried to persuade me to join some sort of English organization, which I refused to do."[7] On the other hand, Hedley's new friends and business colleagues urged him to become an American citizen and told him how to get his first citizenship papers and even taught him answers to questions about the United States government. Hedley admitted that he had gotten a taste of American politics with his arrival during the 1920 Presidential election. He did file his first citizenship papers on September 12, 1922, but was not naturalized until May 3, 1926.[8]

At a later time, Hedley was interviewed by a student as a result of a lecture and made the following comment. "When I first came over in October, 1920,

I made up my mind to like America. I haven't been back in England since. I haven't any desire to go back. America is free and open — everything better. In England there are old customs, old styles. I don't like to meet people from England either. They are not adapted to here. When you talk to them, they start in about England."[9] This perhaps explains why "Scotty" Hedley's Americanization happened so quickly. With this initial receptive attitude, he unhesitatingly embraced American life.

With a successful launch of a Chicago business career as an accountant, Hedley wanted his family to join him. Isabella and the two sons— John Jr. (seven years) and Sidney Roland (one year, nine months) — departed Liverpool on the White Star Steamship Line S. S. *Baltic* on September 10, 1921, with a destination listed as Chicago. They landed at New York on September 20 and, like Hedley, immediately boarded a train for Chicago.[10] The subsequent reunion further cemented the Hedley adaptation to life in the United States. Isabella eventually would become a naturalized citizen on February 9, 1928.[11]

Despite his busy, gainful accountant employment, Hedley decided to obtain a law degree. "In my work as a public accountant 1 have always felt the need of a legal training and I now desire to enter the profession of the law to round out my training as a business executive and counselor."[12] This was his only comment about this new endeavor. He started his law classes at the Chicago Law School on 9 September 1922. For three years he attended classes, from September to early June, allowing him a respite during the summer months. He finally graduated with the degree of L.L.B. on June 10, 1925[13] and then applied for admission to the Chicago Bar. Later, a letter of June 5, 1930, notified him he had been elected a member of the American Bar Association.[14]

In an interview published in an October 29, 1927, Liberty magazine, Hedley proudly summarized his rapid American accomplishments. "I am a lawyer and a certified public accountant, practicing in Chicago; member of the Chicago Bar Association, the Executive Club of Chicago, the High Noon Club of Chicago, Home Lodge, A. F. and A. M., Chicago; the American Society of Certified Public Accountants, the Society of Incorporated Accountants and Auditors, London, England."[15] This statement showed that Hedley was a joiner of organizations, particularly with an eye for those that might be useful in furthering his career.

Just when Hedley's career trajectory seemed to be straight ahead with momentum as a lawyer, accountant, and auditor, a strange one hundred eighty degree turn occurred. It appeared to be related to the *Liberty* magazine article by Floyd Gibbons that established Hedley's title as "The Luckiest Man Alive." The article featured a RAF uniformed Captain J. H. Hedley and a drawing of his feat of falling out of his cockpit and landing on the tail of his same plane. Gibbons included the Hedley story in a series of magazine articles about "The Red Knight of Germany," the World War I exploits of aerial ace Baron von Richthofen. Gibbons believed that Captain R. K. Kirkman and Captain J. H. Hedley's downed plane constituted Richthofen's seventy-second victory. He based this claim on the "English casualty records for that afternoon."[16] Many years later, research would indicate that Richthofen had not shot down Kirkman and Hedley. Hedley, however, in his forthcoming lectures would insist that he was a casualty of the famous Richthofen and that he had battled the Richthofen Circus of fighters on several occasions.

The Gibbons' account about Hedley and his labeling Hedley as "The Luckiest Man Alive" received credible reinforcement by Robert L. Ripley's 1929 book *Believe It or Not*. Ripley, widely known for his cartoons and articles of bizarre items that defied belief, also called Hedley "The Luckiest Man Alive." He stated that his fantastic accident and survival had been authenticated by Hedley's log book and a report filed by "Lieutenant R. C. Purvis, Recording Officer of Twentieth Squadron, R. F. C." Ripley quoted Purvis as saying, "January 6, 1918, Mach. No. 7255. Height, 15,000 ft. Lieutenant Makepeace, M. C., reports Captain J. H. Hedley accidentally thrown into air, afterwards alighted on tail machine and rescued."[17] All this national publicity no doubt convinced Hedley that he should intensify his story telling, lecturing about his now famous adventure, and earn money doing so.

Gibbons wrote in his article, "Hedley's commentaries on his experiences have a rollicking, care-free rhythm, as well becomes the stride of any man who can recount having fallen out of a plane nearly three miles in the air and having fallen back into it. One wonders whether there is any thrill left to which such a man can look forward."[18] But Hedley did find telling his story exhilarating and began speaking tours capitalizing on his new fame. He had given a local talk about his World War I combat as early as 1921 but the new national attention offered far greater opportunities for more intensified lecturing. He developed ways to promote his talks by getting newspapers to take note of his speeches and by preparing and distributing handbills advertising his various appearances. The title of "Luckiest Man Alive" became his motto and his main sales pitch.

In keeping with the best of meticulous bookkeeping, Hedley, for example, kept a beautifully neat ledger detailing his "Schedule of Lectures" for 1928. He recorded the dates, lecture locations, attendance, expenses, fees, and a net profit column. During January, he had ten speaking engagements and a high of seventeen in March with venues ranging from churches to service clubs (Rotary, Kiwanis, Optimists). Individual lecture attendance usually ran from one hundred to three hundred. In July, he participated in a Chautauqua circuit with seventeen different locations and with an estimated attendance total of approximately seven thousand. While his list of expenses was relatively minor, he evidently did not become rich, netting only $1,247.00 during the first seven months. What was surprising, however, was the number of talks he had scheduled. He would scarcely have time for any other business endeavors.[19]

Continued newspaper accounts kept alive and contributed mightily to Hedley's successful speaking events, usually entitled "Rambling Through the Air." For example, The Chicago Herald Examiner of October 12, 1930, included "The Luckiest Man Alive" cartoon.[20] Likewise, The Chicago Daily Times of November 23, 1931, had a "Strange As It Seems" Hedley cartoon.[21] The Milwaukee Journal newspaper of April 21, 1937, featured a two part interview of Hedley discussing his World War I experiences with a prominent cartoon-like drawing entitled "Pitched from Ship at 20,000 Feet, Lives." Notable in The Milwaukee Journal article was a comment that Hedley had come to that city in October 1920 with the intent of killing Captain Charles Niemeyer. Hedley was quoted as saying, "In 1920 I sailed for the United States, reached Milwaukee and, with the help of The Milwaukee Journal, learned that my man had ended his life in Berlin. I was relieved. It was like a reprieve for me. I settled down with my wife in Chicago and became an American citizen."[22] In another writing, Hedley claimed that he had unsuccessfully combed the Milwaukee phone book checking Niemeyer names and the newspaper informed him of the reported Niemeyer suicide. Later in the journal story, the interviewer stated, "After the war, Niemeyer committed suicide in Germany. He was on Lloyd George's list of enemies who should be exterminated because of brutality in handling British prisoners."[23] The Milwaukee newspaper reporter described Hedley as a "Half Pint Ace." "When I met Capt. Hedley in Chicago, I was almost floored. I had expected to find a big strapping fellow with a barrel chest. Instead, I gazed with awe on a little fellow, just 5 feet 1, and now 43 years old, his hair gray. Hedley was unassuming, to say the least."[24] The newspapers, large and small, not only told the Hedley story but also touted his speaking ability. In a presentation to a Galva, Illinois, Chamber of Commerce a newspaper article declared, "Continuing for fully 1 1/2 hours, Captain Hedley held his audience spellbound."[25] Hedley often enlivened his talks with his vision of aviation's future. He made comments about the safety and passenger potential of anticipated aircraft designs. In a speech to the Goodwyn Institute in Memphis, Tennessee, on April 1, 1930, he offered the remarkable idea of "trains of dirigibles, like so many frankfurters linked together" that would carry passengers nonstop from coast to coast by 1950. A Memphis newspaper claimed that Hedley "is a modern Jules Verne prophesying the progress to be made in aviation."[26]

In December of 1933, he was named a Kentucky Colonel, probably as a result of a speaking engagement in that state,[27] and the Robert Ripley "Believe It Or Not" corporation contacted Hedley and invited him to be on a Ripley radio program. He participated in a live radio interview on April 4, 1937. Afterward, Ripley presented a copy of his book to Hedley with the inscription: "To Captain J. H. Hedley 'The Luckiest Man Alive' with ever good wish Ripley 'Believe It or Not' Radio Program, New York, April 4, 1937."[28] This program further strengthened Hedley's fame. The radio transcript and the various newspaper articles told the Hedley story almost word for word, indicating Hedley's numerous repetitions had honed his statements into a set commentary. Nevertheless, his speaking skills, punctuated with humor, entertained and held his audiences.

Although Hedley never departed from his principal occupation of accountant and auditor, supplemented with lecturing, he also had not forsaken aviation. It is not clear if he did much flying but from time to time he had photographs of his visits to an airport flight line, posing with various aircraft. Apparently, he toyed with the idea of linking his flying with some aviation development concepts. On July 9, 1932, Chicago's H. Crossland Pfaff sought to obtain from Hedley written confirmation for what he believed was a verbal agreement with Hedley that he would fly the Crossland Steam Plane, then in construction, on its first flight. Hedley and a Lieutenant Curt W. Prillwitz were "to fly this ship on its first flights, together with the attempt to break the world's endurance non-refueling record, also in the attempt to complete a nonstop flight around the world."[29] While this enterprise came to naught, probably fortunately, Hedley entertained other flying offers. Interestingly, Hedley had another narrow escape in his flying from Chicago to St. Louis. An undated newspaper clipping reported, "Capt. Hedley, now a Chicago lawyer, was forced down near Aurora because of motor trouble. After working on the motor he again took off but had gone only a few hundred yards when the plane crashed. Capt. Hedley climbed from the wreckage, took inventory of his bruises and, finding none of them serious, boarded a train for Chicago."[30]

The stock market crash of 1929, the ensuing financial panic, and the beginning of the Great Depression must have severely curtailed and eventually ended Hedley's prolific lecturing. The lively 1920s had ended. On November 10, 1930, however, John and Isabella welcomed another son, Charles Raymond, who was born in Chicago. This family addition occurred at a time when the Hedleys may have begun experiencing economic problems. Although the family's economic situation was never mentioned, it seems doubtful the Hedleys escaped the troubled times. The collapse of various corporations and businesses surely impacted the need for accountants and auditors. There was a hint of trouble as Hedley evidently sought government employment with an appointment to the Federal Emergency Administration of Public Works in January 1934.[31] Subsequently, photo identification cards indicated that Hedley was "duly authorized to conduct examinations and audits for the Administrator" of this Public Works agency.[32] This was the significant beginning of Hedley's employment by the U. S. Government and no doubt helped to economically sustain the Hedley family during some difficult years.

In another curious twist, he began training with the National College of Massage and Physio-Therapy in Chicago and received a diploma on September 20, 1937. This allowed him to do "Swedish Massage, Medical Gymnastics, Dietetics" and other services. Hedley nowhere indicated whether he pursued and practiced these skills. Much later, however, he showed continued interest in physical and health treatments. In 1946 he obtained a Diploma of Naturopathy from a London Institute of Naturopathy, and in 1954, he had a Diploma in Osteopathy from a Naturopathic and Osteopathic Institute.[33] His motivation for his expanding interest in such subjects was never explained.

Information contained in the 1940 United States census indicated that Hedley's occupation remained auditor but he had been unemployed for four months. He and his family still resided in Chicago.[34] The beginning of the Second World War in 1939 in Europe must have stirred Hedley's deep-seated patriotic and military related feelings. He apparently began looking for ways to aid the Allied cause. He wrote to the Office of Production Management in Washington on January 14, 1941, proposing a plan for improving aircraft production. He was told his ideas had been referred to the Chief of the Air Corps but his plan received no further action.[35] He did secure a role in the American World War II mobilization, however. By the time of his registration for the military draft in early 1942, he had moved to Dayton, Ohio, and gained employment as an auditor for the Army Air Corps Audit Division. This put Hedley into a job associated with his long-term aviation interest. From the beginning, he became a Chicago area auditor with great responsibilities checking important war contracts with such companies as Emerson Electric, Curtiss-Wright, and Allis-Chalmers. He supervised audit operations extending from Chicago to corporation locations from St. Louis, Missouri, to Milwaukee, Wisconsin. In January 1942, Hedley boldly relinquished his Chicago post to take up new but similar duties for the Army Air Corps in east Africa.[36] What prompted this move remains a mystery. Perhaps he was searching for a more direct contribution to the war effort or perhaps he was just ready to undertake a new adventure. Whatever his reason, Hedley sailed from New Jersey on March 21, 1942, on the freight steamer *President Buchanan* and with a stop at Cape Town on April 22 eventually arrived at the Red Sea port of Massaua on 9 May. An eighty mile motor truck trip inland to Asmara ensued with a further motor trip of twenty-five miles to Gura. Hedley reported to Major George T. O'Neill, who was in temporary command of the station.

The Army Air Forces' Audit Residency had been established at Gura, Eritrea, Italian East Africa, on May 10, 1942. The site was in the Middle Eastern Theater of Operations and was also the headquarters of the Army Air Forces 83 Air Depot Group. While some auditors were military men, the audit personnel at the foreign base retained civilian status. John Hedley had a level fourteen rank or "the assimilated rank of Colonel in the U. S. Army" and was Chief Resident Auditor from the inception of the Gura project to January 25, 1944, when he was briefly assigned to Northern Ireland before returning to the United States. Also, he had supervisory jurisdiction of a project in Abadan, Iran, on the Persian Gulf."[37]

Hedley provided precious little detail about his African wartime experience. In a letter to a newspaper reporter, he said, "Right now I'm basking in the shade, perched upon a wooden bench in a shabby little shack set up in the furthermost corner of a 200-acre barren lot, my writing pad suspended upon my knees ..."

"In this tropical location," Hedley continued, "I'm not, as you may guess, taking any active part in actual air fighting in this war. Too old! They tell me. I'm like the old-time ball player sitting on the bench coaching the team along. Recording the strikeouts. Cheering the boys as they run the bases, and clinging — inning after inning — for one more turn at bat." Hedley indicated his loneliness and likely boredom by talking about the joy of getting mail. "Day after day we putter along doing much of the same things over and over again, doing our damnest to 'keep em flying.'" He expressed optimism about the war's progress based on American production. His letter's conclusion revealed a sentiment of many overseas American G. I.s, "The stars stand out in the dark heavens like a million brilliants but all the glamour of this tropical splendor fades into insignificance because we have no white women to gaze upon."[38]

Despite Hedley's relatively mild complaints about his isolated duty, he found time, whether by orders or for pleasure, to travel about in his Middle Eastern world. In October of 1943, he visited the "Holy Sepulcher" in Jerusalem. He also toured Tel-Aviv, Jericho, and Nazareth. On another trip, he went north from Khartoum to Cairo. At another time, he went to Basra and the Anglo-Iranian Oil Company plant at Abadan. He documented his travels with numerous photographs.[39]

With the end of World War II in Europe in May 1945, and the beginning of some demobilization, Hedley's auditor's contract with the Army Air Forces may have neared an end. His employment status at that point remains unclear but he did return to his family in Chicago. Apparently within months, he made a surprising decision to relocate to the Los Angeles, California, area. Hedley failed to explain this distant move west. It is possible, at age fifty-eight, he looked to a future retirement in a pleasant place. Perhaps more likely, however, he had or saw continued employment opportunities with the auditor division of the Army Air Forces in the aircraft industry center of Los Angeles. In 1947, he was working for the Army Audit Agency on Beverly Boulevard in Los Angeles with various auditor assignments in Southern California.[40] Years later, in October 1952, he had identification stating he was a "Staff Auditor, Industrial European District, Auditor General, USAF."[41] This title would seem to indicate Hedley might have had trips to and time in Europe but he did not so record. At this time, blue-eyed, bespectacled Hedley, whose hair had now changed from brown to gray to white, reached the age of sixty-five and seriously weighed and decided on retirement as a government auditor.

Not long after establishing his California residence, he popped back into newspaper notice. The South End Bee, a community newspaper serving the south Los Angeles area, reported on July 21, 1948, that a "Local Essayist Wins $3500." A sub-title of "World War I Close Shave Hits Jackpot" pointed to John H. Hedley at 160 W. 102 Street. Hedley's photograph and "Luckiest Man Alive" story graced the front page. Hedley had won first prize in the "Close Shave" essay contest. "Today after 30 years marriage to Lady Luck, the ex-British airman now a southender is enjoying the dilemma of choosing between a $3500 vacation trip or the same amount in cash — first prize in the Molle-sponsored essay contest in which contestants wrote briefly on 'My Closest Shave.'" Hedley was quoted as saying, "I think I'll take the cash. I've been over most of the world, and anyway, I can use the cash right now."[42]

Scant information about Hedley's activities during his Los Angeles residency prevents a detailed description of the final years in Hedley's life. After the move west, the family—John, Isabella, and the three sons— settled into a rather peaceful and relatively stable existence in southern California. Perhaps John Hedley's military experience had impact on sons Sidney Roland (Rollie) and much younger Charles Raymond (Ray). Sidney Roland enlisted in the Navy in World War II and served as a radio technician on the ship DeHaven. After the war, he married, had two sons (Dennis Roland and Donald Wayne), and took up residence in the Los Angeles area working for Howard Hughes. Charles Raymond lived at home, graduated from Fremont High School in 1949, and then enlisted and began a career in the Marine Corps.[43] Periodic family gatherings occurred at John and Isabella's home and the grandsons fondly remembered their grandfather as loving, caring, and devoted to "Bella."[44]

Hedley's penchant for trying something new did not fade away in California. He went to a chiropractic school, got a license, and had a practice in the Los Angeles area.[45] Also, he attended a barber school, got a license, and did some barbering. He would cut the hair of family members. Besides these enterprises, he became very active in the Masonic Order. Isabella, likewise, participated in the Masonic Eastern Star.[46]

As time went on, John Hedley began to slow down and gradually curtail his activities. For a considerable period, however, he had a daily ritual of walking almost eight blocks to have coffee and a burger. This reflected his long-held concern about staying fit.[47] An individual who tried to correspond with Hedley in 1960 claimed that the Californian refused to discuss details of his wartime service and that he became upset when confronted with his listing of different birth dates. Thus, the now thoroughly retired accountant had indeed changed from the prolific lecturer and ready story teller of earlier years.

On December 20, 1973, wife Isabella died in Los Angeles just short of her 79th birthday.[48] This no doubt had great impact on John Hedley and the Hedley family. Three years later, on April 1, 1977, Captain John Herbert Hedley passed away at age 89. Both Isabella and John were interred at the Inglewood Park Cemetery in the Los Angeles area. Descendants besides the three sons, John Jr., Sidney Roland, and Charles Raymond, included six grandchildren and four great-grandchildren.[49] "The Luckiest Man Alive," flamboyant World War I aerial warrior Captain John Hedley, the excellent story-teller, the man of mysterious and abrupt decisions, the courageous, "Pint Size" bundle of energy, had at last come to rest.

In retrospect, describing the life of John Herbert Hedley proved far easier than explaining it because of its startling paradoxes. First, the small-in-stature Hedley had giant size deeds. From the beginning, he responded to his small size with bantam rooster-type bravery, supreme self-confidence, and even cockiness. He didn't back away from controversy or challenge, whether it be with his military superiors, getting out of the trenches and into flying, or contending with life in a totally new country. Actually his small size may have contributed to his episode of tumbling out of his observer seat but at the same time may have helped him to precariously cling to a plane's fuselage and survive. He consistently turned his diminutive size to advantage in some remarkable accomplishments.

Additionally, there was always the interesting paradox of his deeds mentioned above and his chosen profession as an accountant. Well educated, intelligent young Hedley found success as an accountant and auditor. His neat, carefully organized, beautifully hand-written logs, lecture ledgers, and prison notebooks all revealed a meticulous keeper of business accounts. One normally holds an image of such a businessman as quiet, rather methodical, and a relatively un-adventuresome person. In Hedley's life, he continued to pursue accounting but punctuated his profession with surprising activities, such as a bicycle trooper, volunteering for the infantry, fighting in the trenches, insubordination with military superiors, turning to combat flying, immigrating to the United States, beginning training in law, and volunteering for World War II duty in Africa. Hedley repeatedly plunged into new adventures, surely upsetting any staid accountant's image.

Still another paradox appeared with his sudden decision to immigrate to the United States after World War I. Up to that time, Hedley certainly personified the British aerial warrior and the ambitious, well-schooled citizen of east coast England. He ostensibly had a settled English family life ahead of him. But Hedley abandoned this life course, moved to the United States, and instead embraced becoming a U. S. citizen. He did this intentionally and never looked back.

Hedley's history, at least in what he recorded, was notably a solo history. Rarely did the focus of events stray from Hedley. The available materials, his manuscript, his notebooks, items he collected all kept the spotlight solely on him. There was only an occasional mention of wife Isabella and no comment about his sons. In his earlier years, Hedley did not seem concerned with family matters, thus there was a pronounced void in this aspect of his life. Later in his life in California, this harsh image did seem to soften. Likewise, Hedley only marginally reported on his interactions with his contemporaries. Even with months of prisoner of war time spent together, Hedley failed to discuss any relationship with pilot Kirkman. He neither critiqued nor praised those around him. One can conclude from his writings that Hedley did not emphasize being a team player, although he readily joined in drinking bouts with comrades. No key nor influential people in his life really emerged. As for Hedley himself, he emphasized events and circumstances and avoided conveying emotion, inner thoughts, and motivations for his actions. This proved especially troubling since at various times he impulsively decided to go in a different direction, begging an explanation.

One might assume that devoid of any dialogue or revelations of attitudes, emotions, and sensitive insights, that John Hedley would remain a virtual stick man — a figure lacking full human attributes. That is not the case, however. Hedley's actions and responses to his, at times, unusual challenges and circumstances, created an interesting individual with a very definable character. Clearly, he continually demonstrated courage, both physically and mentally. His World War I combat role, including eleven aerial victories, stands out in this regard. He combined dogged determination with an energetic, spirited drive that led to a pursuit of surprising new endeavors. New directions seemed to develop suddenly at times indicating that feisty Hedley was an impulsive and restless individual. He never was a contemplative person but instead a man of action. This no doubt contributed to his survival at some critical times and helped him hold audiences spellbound during speeches and lectures. From time to time, he displayed loyalty, sincerity, and remarkable optimism. He brought his keen intelligence to bear as he sought to become an American entrepreneur. These characteristics truly made John Hedley a more complex and intriguing individual.

Overall, Captain John Hedley, the "Luckiest Man Alive," had a fast-paced journey through most of his life, with a natural slowing in his senior years. No doubt, he will be remembered forever in history because of his World War I miraculous survival of falling out of his observer cockpit and then landing on the tail of his own aircraft. Certainly, that is the type of event that tends to stick in human memory. But Hedley's legacy extends beyond that one remarkable episode. His life widens our knowledge and understanding of the often neglected role of the observer in World War I aerial combat, helps us better comprehend the trials of the aerial warrior as a prisoner of war, and provides an illuminating account of a post-World War I British RAF captain's transformation into an American citizen.

Chicago businessman Hedley appears in suit and tie and looking as the solid citizen and earnest American auditor and lawyer he had become.

In 1953, Isabella Hedley made a visit to England. This was her British Registration Certificate with the surprisingly only photograph of Hedley's wife contained in his papers.

Hedley entered the Molle shaving cream contest about life's close shaves and won a $3,500 prize. Hedley in the center is flanked on the left by J.W. Swain, a Molle representative, and on the right by Lee Philips, a manager of Owl Sontag drug store at 8719 South Broadway in Los Angeles.

This Captain Hedley photograph appeared in the Liberty magazine article on "The Red Knight of Germany" on October 29, 1927.

ENDNOTES

Preface

1 Stephan Wilkinson, "Amazing But True Stories," Aviation History, May 2014, 33.

Chapter 1

1 Several distributed handbills contained only slight variations. Copies of the handbills can be found in the Hedley Papers in the Lafayette Foundation Archives, Denver, Colorado.

Chapter 2

1 There is considerable confusion about the year of Hedley's birth although the day and month (July 19) remained consistent. The "England and Wales Birth Registration Index, 1837-1920," lists John Herbert Hedley Birth Registration Year 1887, Tynemouth, Northumberland, Vol. 10B, Page 219, Line Number 332. On United States documents related to his becoming an American citizen Hedley indicated the birth year 1890 and on several passports he showed his birth was 1891.

2 Newspaper clipping from unknown newspaper in North Shields, England, date unknown, found in Hedley Papers, Lafayette Foundation Archives, Denver, Colorado.

3 Army Form E. 5012, No. 496, Territorial Force, 4 Years' Service in the United Kingdom, attestation of John Herbert Hedley, Corps: Northern Cyclist Battalion, The National Archives, Kew, London.

4 "The Army Cyclist Corps," The Wartime Memories Project — The Great War, website www.wartime memories project.com.

5 "Back in Britain: Changing Lives at Home in #WW1," http://backinbritain. tumblr.comirss.

6 Ibid.

7 Web Site, "The Long Long Trail—The British Army in the Great War: Was my soldier in the Territorial Force (TF)?" "The recruitment of men into TF units was very localized and remained so well into 1916." With the British World War I declaration of war the TF mobilized for full time service.

8 Army Form E. 5012, No. 496, Territorial Force.

9 Ibid. This age statement is at variance with the date of birth of July 19, 1887.

10 Form: Statement of the Services of No. 496, John Herbert Hedley, 1 May 1915.

11 "Scotty" was often a nickname for Scottish men. Hedley's home indicated his accent may have differed somewhat from other Scots.

12 Hedley Manuscript.

13 Ibid.

14 Ibid. Hedley indicated in a lecture that they had dug some trenches on the sandy beaches and spread some barbed wire entanglements.

15 Ibid.

16 Web Site, The Long Long Trail—The British Army in the Great War: "Was my soldier in the Territorial Force (TF)?"

17 Army Form E. 611, Declaration to be made by a Soldier of the Territorial Force on Re-engagement for the Territorial Force, 29 June 1914.

18 Army Form E. 624, Agreement to be made by an officer or man of the Territorial Force to subject him to liability to serve in any place outside the United Kingdom in the event of National Emergency, 23 September 1914.

19 England and Wales, Marriage Registration Index, 1837-1920.

20 Ibid. Isabella, like her husband, gave a different birth date on occasion. On the U. S. Social Security Index, 1935-2014, and California Death Index, 1940-1997, her birth was indicated as 25 December 1893.

21 Hedley Manuscript.

Chapter 3

1 Hedley Manuscript.

2 This custom, according to Hedley, started with citizens locking their doors at the very end of the year followed by a designated individual then knocking on the door and putting the first foot across the threshold at the beginning of New Year's day. The first-footer needed to be a healthy, good looking male and carrying a piece of coal, money, bread, and salt—symbols of wealth. The first—footer then supposedly brought good luck for the habitants of the house. The first-footer and all the household then joined in toasts and lively celebration.

3 Statement of the Service of No. 496 Name: John Herbert Hedley.

4 Hedley Manuscript.

5 Ibid.

6 Ibid. A story about clothing and leg size can also be found in Lincoln folk-lore.

7 This was a term referring to the rushed expansion of the British Army with the diversity and undisciplined nature of the army's recruits. There was a book with this title.

8 Hedley Manuscript.

9 Ibid.

10 The Salisbury Plain became the army's principal training area. Great Britain needed a large expanse to train thousands of soldiers, particularly room for maneuvers of large units.

11 Hedley Manuscript.

12 Ibid.

13 Daily Orders by Colonel F. B. Toms, Commanding 34th Infantry Base Depot, Etaples, March 9, 1916, 37.

14 Hedley Manuscript.

15 Ibid.

16 Ibid.

17 Ibid.

18 Ibid.

19 Fritz was a common term for Germans and Archie a common name for anti-aircraft fire.

20 Hedley Manuscript.

21 "Show" was a name given to time of aerial combat.

22 Hedley Manuscript.

23 A hand-written form with the heading: "Lieut (Hon Capt) J. H. Hedley R.A.F. late Captain Labor Corps," which reads "Sec Air Ministry forwards Army Form L 3 for above officer for such action as may be considered necessary." A second endorsement read: "Have you any files of the above officer having been transferred or appointed to a temporary commission in the R.A.F., if so will you please state the date of London Gazette this necessary notification appeared in." A note at the end of the page read: "This officer was trsfd to the R.F.C. Gen. List, from 22.12.17 vide L G. 1.2.18."

24 Web Site, The Long, Long Trail—The British Army in the Great War: The Labour Corps of 1917-1918.

25 Canvass became a term associated with the covering of the World War I aircraft. Actually, other textiles may have been used, all generally coated with a dope when stretched on the framework.

Chapter 4

1 Hedley Manuscript.

2 Ibid.

3 Jack Herris and Bob Pearson, Aircraft of World War I, 1914-1918 (London: Amber Books, Ltd., 2010), 46-51.

4 Hedley's "R. F. C. 'Army' Observer Log Book," Army Book 136, in Hedley Papers, Lafayette Foundation Archives, Denver, Colorado.

5 Ibid.

6 Ibid. Hedley's log book indicated he had accumulated 118 hours and 50 minutes of flying time when he left England for France.

7 Jack Herris and Bob Pearson, Aircraft of World War I,1914-1918 (London: Amber Books, Ltd., 2010), 42-43.

8 Ibid, 63, 137. Another source lists the F.2B's top speed as 123 mph.

9 Sometimes the observer was erroneously called an aerial gunner. An aerial

gunner was more often of noncommissioned rank and usually did air fighting.

10 See Samuel Hynes, The Unsubstantial Air: American Fliers in the First World War (New York: Farrar, Straus and Giroux, 2014), 142-145.

11 Hedley Manuscript.

12 Ibid.

13 Ibid.

14 Ibid.

15 Ibid.

16 Ibid.

17 Statement in a Hedley lecture draft. Hedley Papers, Lafayette Foundation Archives, Denver, Colorado

Chapter 5

1 Norman L. R. Franks and Frank W. Bailey, "Top Scorers: The Record of 20 Squadron RFC/RAF," Cross & Cockade, Vol. 4, No. 1, 1973, 32. Also, John Dalling, "A Squadron Saga," Air Classics, December, 1984, 18.

2 Web Site, Winged Sabres: The Stirring Story of 20 Squadron's FE2s and Bristol Fighters Over the Western Front.

3 Franks and Bailey, "Top Scorers: The Record of 20 Squadron RFC/RAF," 32.

4 Hedley Manuscript.

5 Ibid.

6 Ibid.

7 Ibid.

8 Ibid.

9 Franks and Bailey, "Top Scorers: The Record of 20 Squadron, RFC/RAF," 40. Captain Harry George Ernest Luchford was noted for shooting down eleven German aircraft in three months while piloting the F. E. 2D pusher aircraft. He served as a flight commander and received the Military Cross with Bar. He was killed in combat by Walter von Bulow-Bothkamp on December 2, 1917.

10 Hedley log book.

11 British Army Form W3348, 0139, "Combats in the Air," 5 December 1917.

12 British Army Form W3348, 0141, "Combats in the Air," 10 December 1917. Hedley's log book entry indicates this fight took place on December 9.

13 British Army Form W3348, 0142, "Combats in the Air," 22 December 1917. According to Hedley's flight log book this engagement took place on December 18.

14 Franks and Bailey, "Top Scorers: The Record of 20 Squadron, RFC/RAF," 40. The Aerodrome states Makepeace was the pilot for victories three and four.

15 Hedley Manuscript.

Chapter 6

1 Norman L. R. Franks and Frank W. Bailey, "Top Scorers: The Record of 20 Squadron, RFC/RAF," Cross & Cockade, Vol. 4, No. 1, 1973, 32.

2 British Army Form 3348, 0144, "Combats in the Air," 4/1/18. Hedley's log book states this fight occurred on January 3.

3 Comment contained in the text of a Hedley lecture.

4 Hedley manuscript

5 Ibid.

6 This battle account appeared in a three-part The Milwaukee Journal newspaper article of an interview with Hedley by journalist H. H. Steely. The Milwaukee Journal, Milwaukee, Wisconsin, April 21, 1937, 1.

7 This account appeared as a radio script in the Hedley papers. It is undated and contains no information as to when or where it might have been presented. The Milwaukee Journal of April 21, 1937, and other newspapers carried the same story.

8 The Milwaukee Journal, April 21, 1937.

9 Hedley log book.

10 Letter, James Allan, San Francisco, to Captain J. H. Hedley, Chicago, October 25, 1927. This letter is in the Hedley Papers, Lafayette Foundation Archives, Denver, Colorado.

11 Lothrop Stoddard, Luck Your Silent Partner (New York: Horace Liveright, 1929), 124. The source of this comment was not indicated and this remark remains unverified.

12 The Milwaukee Journal, April 21, 1937, 3.

13 Hedley's flying log book had the following statement after the date January 30: "Got in Binge & chased back to France after trouble at Gloucester." Hedley recorded he had 255 hours and 11 minutes time in the air at this point.

14 Hedley Manuscript.

Chapter 7

1 There is some confusion regarding the pilot in this engagement. Although Lt. Thomas Colvill-Jones has been listed as pilot in some documents, Hedley later wrote his pilot was Lt. Makepeace.

2 Hedley Manuscript.

3 Franks and Bailey, "Top Scorers: The Record of the 20th Squadron, RFC/RAF," 40.

4 Hedley Manuscript.

5 Ibid.

6 There is controversy over the pilot for the 17 February 1918 engagement. The "Aerodrome" says that Hedley's pilot was Robert Kirkman.

7 Franks and Bailey, "Top Scorers: The Record of 20 Squadron, RFC/RAF."

8 Hedley Manuscript.

9 Letter, James Allan, San Francisco, to Capt. J. H. Hedley, Chicago, October 25, 1927. This letter is in the Hedley Papers, Lafayette Foundation Archives, Denver, Colorado.

10 John H. Morrow, Jr., German Air Power in World War I (Lincoln: University of Nebraska Press, 1982), 95.

11 David T. Zabeski, Steel Wind: Colonel Georg Bruchmuller and the Birth of Modern Artillery (Westport, Conn.: Praeger, 1994), 72.

12 Martin Middlebrook, The Kaiser's Battle (London: Penguin Books, Ltd., 1978), 279-80.

13 British Army Form W. 334T8, "Combats in the Air," 23/3/18.

14 The 6 January 1919 citation, Order 12738, can be found in the Hedley Pa-

pers, Lafayette Foundation Archives, Denver, Colorado.

15 The Milwaukee Journal, April 21, 1937, 3.

16 John Toland, No Man's Land:1918:The Last Year of the Great War (Garden City, New York: Doubleday, 1980), 87.

17 Hedley Manuscript.

18 Ibid.

19 Franks and Bailey, "Top Scorers: The Record of 20 Squadron, RFC/RAF," 40.

20 Hedley Manuscript.

21 Ibid.

22 Ibid.

23 Some newspaper accounts listed Captain Kirkman's name as Kirkham.

24 James Streckfuss, "Flying with 20: The Wartime Experiences of John Metcalf Purcell," Over the Front, Vol. 2, #1 (Spring 1987), 55.

25 Diary-like book in the Hedley Papers, Lafayette Foundation Archives, Denver, Colorado.

26 Hedley Manuscript.

27 Diary-like book in the Hedley Papers, Lafayette Foundation Archives, Denver, Colorado.

28 Ibid. There is a major discrepancy between this account which Hedley wrote and no doubt presented in his lectures and a document comment he signed upon his repatriation on 16/12/1918. The hand-written statement said "On returning from low flying bombing and shooting troops and transport we were attacked by an Albatros. Fought & brought him down with observer's gun. Both petrol tanks shot through and unable to get home landed 20 yds in front of German advancing front line. Machine gun fire from ground kept at us until we actually left the machine—unable to fire the machine." This comment "unable to fire the machine" seemed to contradict earlier reports of the plane's destruction by fire.

29 After the war, Gallwitz would be a professor of agricultural machinery at the University of Gottingen from 1936 to 1965.

30 Franks and Bailey, "Top Scorers: The Record of 20 Squadron, RFC/RAF," 43. At one time, one of the members of 20 Squadron was Canadian-born

Captain Harold Hartney. Hartney would become a member of the United States Air Service, get promoted to Lt. Colonel, and made commander of the 1st Pursuit Group near the end of the war.

31 Hedley in his lectures and writings often claimed he had 12 aircraft victories and one balloon, had 53 air fights, and was wounded three times.

Chapter 8

1 Hedley Manuscript.

2 Ibid.

3 Pocket-size Diary, "Notiz-Buch," contained in the Hedley Papers, Lafayette Foundation Archives, Denver, Colorado.

4 Hedley Manuscript.

5 Ibid. The RE.8, with a crew of 2, had a maximum speed of 98 mph and a service ceiling of 11,000 feet. See Jack Herris and Bob Pearson, Aircraft of World War I, 1914-1918 (London: Amber Books, Ltd., 2010), 142.

6 Pocket-size Diary.

7 Ibid.

8 Letter, Major E. H. Johnston, 20 Squadron, to Mrs. J. H. Hedley, North Shields, England, postmarked 5 April 1918, Hedley Papers, Lafayette Foundation Archives, Denver, Colorado.

9 Pocket-size Diary.

10 Ibid.

11 Hedley Manuscript.

12 Ibid.

13 Ibid.

14 Pocket-size Diary.

15 Hedley Manuscript.

16 Ibid.

17 H. G. Durnford, The Tunnellers of Holzminden (New York: Penguin Books, 1940), 116.

18 Pocket-size Diary.

19 The ten escapees eventually received medals from King George V at Buckingham Palace.

20 Durnford, The Tunnellers of Holzminden, 116-117.

21 Ibid.

22 Pocket-size Diary.

23 Ibid.

24 Notebook kept by Hedley, Hedley Papers, Lafayette Foundation Archives, Denver, Colorado.

25 Ibid.

26 Durnford, The Tunnellers of Holzminden, 98.

27 Hedley Sketch Book, Hedley Papers, Lafayette Foundation Archives, Denver, Colorado.

28 Pocket-size Diary.

29 The Sketch Book section "Barbedwireitis" was listed as from "Zuricher Zeitung" of July 1918 and quoted a Dr. Vischer. The Sketch Book, Hedley Papers, Lafayette Foundation Archives, Denver, Colorado.

30 Hedley Manuscript.

31 Hedley Sketch Book.

32 Hedley Manuscript.

33 Ibid.

34 Hedley Sketch Book.

35 Captain John H. Hedley Service Record, The National Archives.

36 The port of Hull is on one side of an over a mile-wide tidal river and Grimsby is on the other side. A ferry ran between Hull and Grimsby.

37 Letter contained in Hedley Papers, Lafayette Foundation Archives, Denver, Colorado.

38 This document can be found in the Hedley Papers, Lafayette Foundation Archives, Denver, Colorado.

Chapter 9
1 Protection Certificate (Officer), 26.2.19, The National Archives.

2 Handwritten note outlining his auditor years with several firms, Hedley Papers, Lafayette Foundation Archives, Denver, Colorado.

3 Grandson Don Hedley believes Hedley's father told his son he should go to America. Interview author with Don Hedley, September 1, 2015.

4 Hedley Manuscript.

5 Ibid.

6 A Galva, Illinois, newspaper stated Hedley came from "East Moline, where he was in charge of the recent reorganization of the R. & V. Engineering Company." Newspaper clipping in the Hedley file.

7 Hedley Manuscript.

8 Certificate of Naturalization No. 2330962 Petition Vol.188, No. 21515, issued May 3, 1926.

9 Unknown student in an interview of Captain J. H. Hedley published in Richmond High School Echo'31, undated, Richmond, Missouri. Clipping in Hedley Papers, Lafayette Foundation Archives, Denver, Colorado.

10 Preliminary Form for Petition for Naturalization, Department of Labor, Naturalization Service, April 30, 1927.

11 U. S. Department of Labor, Immigration and Naturalization Service Certificate P46252 C2722819, February 9, 1928.

12 Undated handwritten note contained in the Hedley Papers, Lafayette Foundation Archives, Denver, Colorado.

13 Application of John Herbert Hedley for Admission to the Bar, Certificate of Attendance at Law School, June 9, 1926.

14 Letter, American Bar Association, Chicago, Illinois, June 5, 1930, to John Herbert Hedley, Chicago, Illinois, Hedley Papers, Lafayette Foundation Archives, Denver, Colorado.

15 Floyd Gibbons, "Richthofen 'Shoots a Triple' and Gets Another Medal — The Luckiest Man Alive Tells His Tale," Part Twenty of "The Red Knight of Germany," Liberty, October 29, 1927, 53-57.

16 Ibid., 54.

17 Robert L. Ripley, Believe It or Not (New York: Simon and Schuster, 1929), 54.

18 Ibid., 55.

19 Hedley ledger sheets, Schedule of Lectures 1928, Hedley Papers, Lafayette Foundations Archives, Denver, Colorado.

20 The Chicago Herald Examiner, Chicago, Illinois, October 12, 1930.

21 The Chicago Daily Times, Chicago, Illinois, November 23, 1931.

22 The Milwaukee Journal, Milwaukee, Wisconsin, Part II, April 22, 1937.

23 The Milwaukee Journal, Milwaukee, Wisconsin, Part I, April 21, 1937, 13. The story of Niemeyer's suicide circulated but was never confirmed. When the Armistice came, Niemeyer disappeared. Some believed he fled in some sort of disguise. A number of prisoners believed he could have been tried for war crimes. Also, there was the thought that an avenger had killed him.

24 Ibid., 1.

25 Unidentified March 17, 1922, newspaper clipping in Hedley Papers, Lafayette Foundation Archives, Denver, Colorado.

26 Memphis Press-Scimitar, Memphis, Tennessee, April 1, 1930, 1.

27 Ruby Lafoon, Governor of Kentucky, Captain H. Hedley Chicago, Illinois, appointed as Aide-de-Camp on the Governor's Staff with the rank and grade of Colonel.

28 The inscribed Ripley book is contained in the Hedley Papers, Lafayette Foundation Archives, Denver, Colorado.

29 Letter from H. Crossland Pfaff, Chicago, Illinois, to Captain J. H. Hedley, Chicago, Illinois, July 9, 1932. Letter is contained in the Hedley Papers, Lafayette Foundation Archives, Denver, Colorado.

30 Unidentified, undated newspaper clipping in Hedley Papers, Lafayette Foundation Archives, Denver, Colorado.

31 Letter from Senator J. Hamilton Lewis, Chicago, Illinois, to Colonel J. H. Hedley, Chicago, Illinois, January 5, 1934, contained in the Hedley Papers, Lafayette Foundation Archives, Denver, Colorado.

32 Several photo identification cards were issued to Hedley by the Federal Emergency Administration of Public Works Accounting Division. This agency was one of President Franklin D. Roosevelt's depression era organizations authorized by the National Industrial Recovery Act of June 16, 1933. Card No. 117 had no date but said "Void after 6/30/ 34." Card No. 50 was dated 1934-35 and Card No. 358 stated "This authority expires June 30, 1937."

33 The Diploma of the National College of Massage and PhysioTherapy, Chicago, Illinois, September 20, 1937; The Diploma of Naturopathy from the British Institute of Naturopathy, London, October 31 1946; and the Diploma in Osteopathy from Naturopathic and Osteopathic Institute, June 23, 1954, are in the Hedley Papers, Lafayette Foundation Archives, Denver, Colorado.

34 1940 United States Census.

35 Letter from Office of Production Management, Washington, D. C., to Mr. J. H. Hedley, March 6, 1941, Hedley Papers, Lafayette Foundation Archives, Denver, Colorado.

36 A brief, typed government document outlined the history of Hedley's Gura assignment. The document is contained in the Hedley Papers, Lafayette Foundation Archives, Denver, Colorado. Hedley's departure from Chicago Area Auditor duties prompted letters of regret and yet of appreciation for his serving overseas by some of his business associates and clients. Some of these letters are in the Hedley Papers.

37 Ibid. Identification card No. 11973, Cairo, 1 July 1943, stated: "This certifies that John H. Hedley, Chief Auditor, U.S.A.A.F., has the assimilated rank of Colonel in the U. S. Army, and is authorized to wear officer's uniform without insignia." A photo identification card, dated 11 October 1943, gave Hedley authority over all the Middle East.

38 Undated letter from John H. Hedley to Mrs. Rosborough for a unidentified newspaper column "Letters from Our Boys" in Hedley Papers, Lafayette Foundation Archives, Denver, Colorado.

39 Grandson Don Hedley remembered a leopard skin rug in his grandfather's home. It probably was a trophy from his African-Middle East time.

40 The Army Audit Agency identification card No. 132, dated 1 February 1947, gave his work address as 3636 Beverly Blvd, Los Angeles, California.

41 Identification Card No. 183, Department of the Air Force, Office of the Auditor General, Staff Auditor, Industrial European District, Auditor General, USAF, dated 28 October 1952. Hedley also had a "European Command Motor Vehicle License K2-5571, Hq. USAFE Auditor General E-066377 issued 8 January 1953.

42 The South End Bee, Los Angeles, California, July 21, 1948, 1, 9, 14. The paper stated that Hedley's son Charles Raymond was a student at Fremont High School.

43 Son Charles Raymond, apparently with more of a young, rebellious temperament, did not always join in family gatherings. After joining the Marine Corps, he became a Hawaii resident.

44 Interview author with Don Hedley, September 1, 2015.

45 Interview author with Dennis Hedley, August 29, 2015.

46 Interview author with Don Hedley, September 1, 2015.

47 Ibid.

48 The California Death Index, 1940-1997. This document incorrectly listed her birthdate as 25 December 1893.

49 John Herbert Hedley obituary, The Los Angeles Times, April 2, 1977.

BIBLIOGRAPHY

Anders, Curtis. *Fighting Airmen*. New York: Putnam, 1966.

Archibald, Norman. *Heaven High, Hell Deep*. New York: Albert & Charles Boni, 1935.

Army Times Editors. *Famous Fighters of World War I*. New York: Dodd, Mead, 1964.

Army War College. *The Signal Corps and the Air Service, 1917-1918*. Washington DC: Government Printing Office, 1922.

Baldwin, Hanson W. *World War I*. New York: Grove Press, 1949.

Ballard, Jack Stokes. *The 147th Aero Squadron in World War I: A Training and Combat History of the "Who Said Rats" Squadron*. Atglen, PA: Schiffer Publishing Ltd., 2013.

Ballard, Jack Stokes. *War Bird Ace: The Great War Exploits of Capt. Field E. Kindley*. College Station, TX: Texas A & M University Press, 2007.

Baring, Maurice. *Flying Corps Headquarters, 1914-1918*. London: William Blackwood & Sons, 1968.

Barker, Ralph. *The Royal Flying Corps in France: From Mons to the Somme*. London: Constable, 1994.

Barker, Ralph. *The Royal Flying Corps in France: From Bloody April 1917 to Final Victory*. London: Constable, 1995.

Barnett, Correlli. *The Sword Bearers: Supreme Command in the First World War*. New York: Signet Books, 1963.

Berry, Henry. *Make the Kaiser Dance*. Garden City, NY: Doubleday, 1978.

Biddle, Maj. Charles J. *Fighting Airmen: The Way of the Eagle*. Garden City, NY: Doubleday, 1968.

Biddle, Tami. "A Learning in Real Time: The Development and Implementation of Air Power in the First World War," Air Power History: Turning Points from Kitty Hawk to Kosovo, ed. Sebastian Cox and Peter Gray. Portland, OR: Frank Cass, 2002.

Bingham, Hiram. *An Explorer in the Air Service*. New Haven, CT: Yale University Press, 1920.

Bishop, William A. *The Courage of the Early Morning*. New York: David McKay Co., 1966.

Bowen, Ezra, et al. *Knights of the Air*. Alexandria, VA: Time-Life Books, 1980.

Bowyer, Chaz. *The Age of the Biplane*. Englewood Cliffs, NJ: Prentice-Hall, 1981.

Boyes. *Airmen of World War I*. London: Arms & Armour Press, 1975.

Boyle, Andrew. *Trenchard, Man of Vision*. London: Collins, 1962.

Boyne, Walter J. *The Influence of Air Power upon History*. Gretna, LA: Pelican Publishing, 2003.

Bradshaw, Stanley. *Flying Memories*. London: John Hamilton, 1935.

Brewer, Leighton. *Riders of the Sky*. New York: Houghton Mifflin, 1934.

Briscoe, W. A. and H. R. Stanard. *Capt. Ball. V. C.* London: Herbert Jenkins, Ltd., 1938.

Bruce, J. M. *Warplanes of the First World War, Fighters Volume IV and V*. Garden City, NY: Doubleday, 1972.

Budiansky, Stephen. *Air Power: The Men, Machines, and Ideas That Revolutionized War from Kitty Hawk to the Gulf War II*. New York: Viking, 2004.

Burlingame, Roger. *General Billy Mitchell, Champion of Air Defense*. New York: McGraw-Hill, 1952.

Callender, Gordon, Jr. and Gordon Callender Sr., eds. *War in an Open Cockpit: The Wartime Letters of Captain Alvin Andrew Callender, R.A.F.* West Roxbury, Mass: World War I Aero, 1978.

Campbell, Christopher. *Aces and Aircraft of World War I*. Poole, Dorset, U. K.: Blandford Press, Ltd., 1981.

Chant, Christopher. *A Century of Triumph: A History of Aviation*. New York: Free Press, 2002.

Christy, Joe and Page Shamburger. *Aces and Planes of World War I*. New York: Sports Car Press, Ltd., 1968.

Clapp, Frederick M. *A History of the 17th Aero Squadron*. Garden City. NY: Country Life Press, 1920.

Clark, Alan. *Aces High: The War in the Air Over the Western Front*. New York: G. P. Putnam, 1973.

Codman, Charles. *Contact*. Boston: Little, Brown, 1937.

Coffman, Edward M. *The War to End All Wars*. Madison, WI: University of Wisconsin Press, 1986.

Collishaw, Raymond. *Air Command: A Fighter Pilot's Story*. London: William Kimber, 1973.

Conover, Harvey. *Diary of a World War I Pilot*. Spokane, WA: Conover-Patterson, 2004.

Cook, Jacqueline. *The Real Great Escape*. North Sidney, Australia: Random House, 2013.

Cooke, James J. *The U. S. Air Service in the Great War, 1917-1919*. Westport, CT: Praeger, 1996.

Coppens, Willy. *Flying in Flanders*. New York: Ace Books, 1971.

Cuneo, John R. *The Air Weapon, 1914-1916: Vol. II of Winged Mars*. Harrisburg, PA: Military Service Publishing, 1947.

Dalling, John. "A Squadron Saga," Air Classics. December 1984.

Daso, Dik Alan. *Hap Arnold and the Evolution of American Airpower*. Washington, DC: Smithsonian Press, 2000.

Douglas, Sholto. *Combat and Command*. New York: Simon & Schuster, 1963.

Driggs, Laurence LaTourette. *Heroes of Aviation*. Boston: Little, Brown, 1936.

Durnford, H. G. *The Tunnellers of Holzminden*. New York: Penguin Books, 1940.

Elliott, Stuart E. *Wooden Crates and Gallant Pilots*. Philadelphia: Dorrance & Co., 1974.

Fitzsimons, Bernard. *Warplanes and Air Battles of World War I*. New York: Beekman House, 1973.

Flammer, Philip M. *The Vivid Air: The Lafayette Escadrille*. Athens: University of Georgia Press, 1981.

Fonck, Captain Rene. *Ace of Aces*. Garden City, NY: Doubleday, 1967.

Franks, Norman. *Aircraft versus Aircraft: The Illustrated Story of Fighter Pilot Combat since 1914*. New York: Macmillan, 1986.

Franks, Norman. *Dog-Fight: Aerial Tactics of the Aces of World War I*. London: Greenhill Books, 2003.

Franks, Norman and Frank W. Bailey. "Top Scorers: The Record of 20 Squadron RFC/RAF," Cross & Cockade. Vol. 4, No. 1, 1973.

Franks, Norman, Frank W. Bailey, and Russell Guest. *Above the Lines: The Aces and Fighter Units of the German Air Service*. London: Grub Street, 1993.

Fredericks, Pierce G. *The Great Adventure: America in the First World War*. New York: Ace Books, 1960.

Funderburk, Thomas R. *The Early Birds of War: The Daring Pilots and Fighter Aeroplanes of World War I*. New York: Grosset & Dunlap, 1968.

Funderburk, Thomas R. *The Fighters: The Men and Machines of the First World War*. New York: Grosset & Dunlap, 1965.

Russell, Paul. *The Great War and Modern Memory*. London: Oxford University Press, 1975.

Gibbons, Floyd. "Richthofen 'Shoots a Triple' and Gets Another Medal — The Luckiest Man Alive Tells His Tale," Part Twenty of "The Red Knight of Germany," Liberty. October, 1927.

Gibbons, Floyd. *The Red Knight of Germany*. Garden City, NY: Garden City Publishing, 1927.

Gilbert, Martin. *The First World War*. New York: Henry Holt, 1994.

Gordon, Arthur. *The American Heritage History of Flight*. New York: American Heritage, 1962.

Gordon, Denis. *The Lafayette Flying Corps. The American Volunteers in the French Air Service in World War One*. Atglen, PA: Schiffer Publishing Ltd., 2000.

Gray, Peter and Owen Thetford. *German Aircraft of the First World War*. London: Putnam, 1962.

Green, William and Gordon Swanborough, eds. *An Illustrated Anatomy of the World's Fighters: The Inside Story of over 100 Classics in the Evolution of Fighter Aircraft*. St. Paul, Minn.: MB1 Publishing, 2001.

Grinnell-Milne, Duncan. *Wind in the Wires*. Garden City, NY: Doubleday, 1968.

Gurney, Gene. *Flying Aces of World War I*. New York: Scholastic Book Services, 1965.

Guttman, Jon. *USAS 1st Pursuit Group*. Oxford: Osprey Publishing, 2008.

Hallion, Richard P. *Rise of Fighter Aircraft, 1914-1918*. Annapolis, MD: Nautical & Aviation Publishing Company of America. 1984.

Hallion, Richard P. *Strike from the Sky: The History of Battlefield Air Attack, 1911- 1945*. Washington, DC: Smithsonian Press, 1989.

Hanson, Neil. *Escape from Germany*. London: Doubleday, 2011.

Harris, John N. *Knights of the Air, Canadian Aces of WWI*. New York: St. Martin's Press, 1958.

Hartney, Harold E. *Up and At Em: Memoirs of an American Air Ace.* Garden City, NY: Doubleday, 1971.

Hegener, Henri. *Fokker — The Man and the Aircraft.* Los Angeles, CA: Aero Publishers, 1961.

Herris, Jack and Bob Pearson. *Aircraft of World War I, 1914-1918.* London: Amber Books, 2010.

Higham, Robin. *100 Years of Air Power and Aviation.* College Station, TX: Texas A & M University Press, 2003.

Holley, I. B. Jr. *Ideas and Weapons: Exploitation of the Aerial Weapon in the United States during World War I: A Study in the Technological Advance, Military Doctrine, and Development of Weapons.* New Haven, CT: Yale University Press, 1953.

Howard, Michael. *The First World War.* Oxford: Oxford University Press, 2002.

Hudson, James J. *In Clouds of Glory.* Fayetteville, AR: University of Arkansas Press, 1990.

Hynes, Samuel. *The Unsubstantial Air: American Fliers in the First World War.* New York: Farrar, Straus and Giroux, 2014.

Imrie, Alex. *Pictorial History of the German Air Service, 1914-1918.* Chicago: Henry Regnery, 1973.

Jackson, Robert. *Fighter Pilots of World War I.* New York: St. Martin's Press, 1977.

Jane's Fighting Aircraft of World War I. London: Random House Group, 2001.

Johnson, J. E. *Full Circle: The Tactics of Air Fighting, 1914-1964.* New York: Ballantine, 1964.

Jones, H. A. *The Official History of the War in the Air.* London: Imperial War Museum, 1921.

Keegan, John. *The First World War.* New York: Alfred A. Knopf, 1999.

Kennett, Lee. *The First Air War, 1914-1918.* New York: Free Press, 1991.

Kent, Zachary. *World War I: The War to End Wars.* Hillside, NJ: Enslow Publishers, 1994.

Kilduff, Peter. *Over the Battlefront.* London: Arms and Armour Press, 1996.

Kilduff, Peter. *Richthofen: Beyond the Legend of the Red Baron.* New York: John Wiley & Sons, 1993.

King, Jere Clemens. *The First World War.* New York: Harper & Row, 1972.

Lee, Arthur Gould. *No Parachute: A Fighter Pilot in World War I.* New York: Harper & Row, 1970.

Lengel, Edward G. *To Conquer Hell: The Meuse-Argonne, 1918.* New York: Henry Holt and Company, 2008.

Libby, Frederick. *Horses Don't Fly.* New York: Arcade Publishing, 2000.

Liddell Hart, Captain B. H. *The Real War, 1914-1918.* Boston: Little, Brown, 1930.

Longstreet, Stephen. *The Canvas Falcons: The Men and the Planes of World War I.* New York: Barnes & Noble Books, 1970.

Maitland, Lester J. *Knights of the Air.* Garden City, NY: Doubleday, Doran, 1929.

Mason, Francis K. *Aces of the Air.* New York: Mayflower Books, 1981.

Mason, Herbert Molloy, Jr. *High Flew the Falcons: The French Aces of World War I.* Philadelphia, PA: J. B. Lippincott, 1965.

Mason, Herbert Molloy, Jr. *The Lafayette Escadrille.* New York: Random House, 1964.

McConnell, James R. *Flying for France.* New York: Grosset & Dunlap, 1916.

McKee, Alexander. *The Friendless Sky: The Story of Air Combat in World War I.* New York: William Morrow, 1964.

Memphis Press - Scimitar., 1930.

Middlebrook, Martin. *The Kaiser's Battle.* London: Penguin Books, Ltd., 1978.

Morrow, John H. Jr. *The Great War in the Air: Military Aviation from 1909 to 1921.* Washington, DC: Smithsonian Press, 1992.

Morrow, John H. Jr. *German Air Power in World War I.* Lincoln: University of Nebraska

Mortimer, Gavin. *The First Eagles: The Fearless American Aces Who Flew with the RAF in World War I.* Minneapolis, MN: Zenith Press, 2014.

Munson, Kenneth. *Fighters 1914-19.* New York: Macmillan, 1968.

Neumann, Maj. Georg Paul, ed. *The German Air Force in the Great War.* Translated by J. E. Gurdon. Portway, Bath, U. K.: Cedric Chivers, Ltd., 1969.

Nordhoff, C. B. and James N. Hall. *Falcons of France.* Boston: Little, Brown, 1936.

Norman, Aaron. *The Great Air War.* New York: Macmillan, 1968.

Parsons, Edwin C. *I Flew with the Lafayette Escadrille.* Indianapolis, IN: E. C. Seale Co., 1963.

Platt, Frank C. *Great Battles of World War I: In the Air.* New York: Weathervane Books, 1966.

Reynolds, Quentin. *They Fought for the Sky*. New York: Bantam Books, 1957.

Richthofen, Manfred von. *The Red Baron*. Translated by Peter Kilduff. Garden City, NY: Doubleday, 1969.

Rickenbacker, Captain Eddie V. *Fighting the Flying Circus*. Garden City, NY: Doubleday, 1965.

Ripley, Robert L. *Believe It or Not*. New York: Simon and Schuster, 1929.

Robertson, Bruce, ed. *Air Aces of the 1914-1918 War*. Los Angeles, CA: Aero Publishers, 1962.

Robinson, Douglas. *Giants in the Sky*. Seattle, WA: University of Washington Press, 1973.

Rogers, Bogart. *A Yankee Ace in the RAF*. Lawrence, KS: University Press of Kansas, 1996.

Rowe, Josiah P. *Letters from a World War I Aviator*. Boston: Sinclaire, 1986.

Simkins, Peter. *Air Fighting 1914-1918*. London: Imperial War Museum, 1978.

Sims, Edward H. *Fighter Tactics and Strategy, 1914-1970*. New York: Harper & Row, 1972.

Smithers, A. J. *Wonder Aces of the Air: The Flying Heroes of the Great War*. London: Gordon & Cremonesi, 1980.

Spick, Mike. *The Ace Factor: Air Combat and the Role of Situational Awareness*. Shrewsbury, U. K.: Airlife Publishing, 1988.

Stallings, Lawrence. *The Doughboys*. New York: Harper & Row, 1963.

Stoddard, Lothrop. *Luck Your Silent Partner*. New York: Horace Liveright, 1929.

Stokesbury, James L. *A Short History of Air Power*. New York: William Morrow, 1986.

Stokesbury, James L. *A Short History of World War I*. New York: William Morrow, 1981.

Strachan, Hew. *The First World War*. New York: Viking Penguin, 2004.

Strachan, Hew, ed. *World War I: A History*. Oxford: Oxford University Press, 1998.

Streckfuss, James. "Flying with 20: The Wartime Experiences of John Metcalf Purcell," Over the Front. Vol. 1, No. 1, Spring 1987.

Sumner, Ian. *German Air Forces 1914-1918*. Oxford: Osprey Publishing, Ltd., 2005.

The Chicago Daily Times. 1931.

The Chicago Herald Examiner 1930.

The Los Angeles Times. 1977.

The Milwaukee Journal. 1937.

The South End Bee. (Los Angeles). 1948.

Toland, John. *No Man's Land:1918: The Last Year of the Great War*. Garden City, NY: Doubleday, 1980.

Toliver, Col. Raymond F. and Trevor J. Constable. *Fighter Aces*. New York: Macmillan, 1965.

Udet, Ernst. *Ace of the Iron Cross*. Garden City, NY: Doubleday, 1970.

Villard, Henry S. *Contact! The Story of the Early Birds*. Washington, DC: Smithsonian Press, 1987.

Whitehouse, Arch. *Legion of the Lafayette*. Garden City, NY: Doubleday, 1962.

Wilkinson, Stephan. "Amazing But True Stories," Aviation History. May 2014.

Wise, S. F. *Canadian Airmen and the First World War. Vol. I*. Toronto: Toronto University Press, 1980.

Woodhouse, Jack. *The War in the Air, 1914-1918*. London: Almark Publishing, 1974.

Woodman, Harry. *Early Aircraft Armament: The Aeroplane and Its Gun up to 1918*. Washington, DC: Smithsonian Press, 1989.

Wukovits, John F. *World War I Flying Aces*. San Diego, CA: Lucent Books, 2002.

Yeats, V. M. *Winged Victory*. London: Jonathan Cape, 1934; reprint 1961.

Zabecki, David T. *Steel Wind: Colonel Georg Bruchrnuller and the Birth of Modern Artillery*. Westport, CT: Praeger, 1994.

INDEX

T

CPSIA information can be obtained
at www.ICGtesting.com
Printed in the USA
BVHW04s1302240918
528355BV00011B/124/P

9 781480 941526